ST MARTIN'S
TRUE CRIME
CLASSICS

Susan's resentment towards her husband Jim seemed to be increasing on virtually a daily basis. One time, a couple of friends called round to drop off some scuba gear they had borrowed and witnessed firsthand the tensions between Susan and Jim when the couple started screaming at one another about some petty point.

In the middle of that particular row, Jim jokingly suggested his wife hire a hitman if she was so cheesed off with him. Susan screamed back that he would probably miss anyhow. Jimmy Grund then said that if someone was going to succeed they should shoot their victim in the eye because of the thin bone structure in that area. Susan Grund looked over at her husband with an intrigued expression on her face. "Really," she thought to herself. "That is very interesting."

# DEADLY SEDUCTION

## WENSLEY CLARKSON

St. Martin's Paperbacks

*To Toby, Polly, Rosie, and Fergus*

# Notes of Gratitude

The idea of using a leaden, dispassionate word like "acknowledgments" for this section cannot begin to express the depth of my feelings for the many individuals who have made this book possible. I owe them my deepest and most heartfelt gratitude.

First to my agent Peter Miller and my editor Charles Spicer. Without them this book would never have happened. Their support and guidance has been very much appreciated. Also, many, many thanks to Frank Abatemarco, whose investigative skills proved invaluable.

Then there are the townsfolk of Peru, Indiana, who welcomed me with such enthusiasm and hospitality. They include: James A. Grund, Connie Grund, Gary Nichols, Wil Siders, Bob Brinson, Mary Heltzel, Charlie Scruggs, Don Fern, Darlene Worden, Nellie Sanders, Jane Allen, Tony Hare, Mary Sue Frietag, Jack and Linda Rich, Anne Hubbard, Nancy Newman, Aimi Bell, Shirley Day, and the staff of the Rosewood Mansion Bed and Breakfast.

In Oklahoma City there was: J. M. Einhorn, Don Deason, Lester Suenram, Paddy Harkey, Vivian Susil.

But one of my biggest debts of gratitude must go to Andy Pierce at the *Peru Daily Tribune*.

Lastly, a special word of thanks to Joe Paolella, whose expertise proved invaluable, and Mark Sandelson for providing all the usual facilities.

# Author's Note

The central figure in this story, Susan Grund, changed her name frequently through her propensity for marriage. In an effort to avoid confusion, throughout the book she is referred to by whichever name she was using at the time.

Some of the dialogue represented in this book was constructed from available documents, some was drawn from courtroom testimony, and some was reconstituted from the memory of participants.

Every unhappy family is unhappy in its own way
—*Leo Tolstoy*

# Prologue

The cold, steel nozzle of the semiautomatic pressed hard against Jimmy Grund's eyelid, then the killer squeezed the trigger. Grund did not even have time to awaken from his slumber. If he had, he would have looked up and recognized the face above him immediately. There was no struggle. The bullet entered the left corner of Grund's eye, traveled through his brain, exited the right side of the back of the head, and embedded itself in the base of the couch's armrest. His life was snuffed out in a split second.

Susan Grund entered the bedroom of her vast mansion and saw the corpse of her husband, Jimmy. He looked so relaxed. His legs were crossed and he was sitting at his favorite angle on the sofa in the bedroom he shared with her. His left arm lay across his chest. He was still dressed in his favorite green golf shirt and in his right hand he clutched a Kleenex tissue. He looked very peaceful. There was no sign of a struggle.

Then she saw the gunshot wound to his left eye and a drop of blood on his mouth.

On the floor was a personal check made out for two hundred and ninety-five dollars. Handwritten notes were sprawled across the coffee table in front of him. They looked like the outline for a speech he was planning to make.

A TV remote sat on the sofa next to Jimmy Grund. His eyeglasses sat on the coffee table. It all had the ring of comfort to it. No struggle. No pain. No anguish.

Susan Grund leaned down to touch him. There was no response. She then called out to him, "Jim? Jim?" Nothing.

"It's my husband, we just got here, and there's blood on him," Susan Grund explained breathlessly after dialing 911.

She went on to inform the Dukes Memorial Hospital Emergency Room that she had found her husband shot in the bedroom of their house. They had to come quickly.

The hospital immediately contacted the Peru, Indiana, Police Department, which got in touch with the Miami County Sheriff's Department because the Grund house was outside of the city limits.

Downstairs in the basement of the house, Susan's seven-year-old daughter Tanelle, and her cousin Andrea had been awoken from their sleepover by the sound of Susan crying and talking on the telephone. They walked up the stairs bleary eyed and asked her what was happening.

At the hospital, the dispatcher heard Susan Grund tell one of the children. "Daddy's not well right now."

Then she spoke softly into the receiver, "Oh God, please hurry. . . ."

Susan stayed on the line to the dispatcher, opened the front door, and turned on the outside lights to the house and waited in the warm summer night air for the ambulance to appear. The mobile phone was still glued to her ear as the white paramedics vehicle slid to a halt on the gravel-covered drive a few minutes later, at 11:58 P.M.

Dukes Memorial Hospital emergency medical technician Carolyn Shaffer immediately went to the bedroom. As she walked in the room, the first thing she noticed were suitcases sprawled across the bed, then she turned and saw the corpse of Jimmy Grund. She did not need to check his pulse to know he had already gone. But Shaffer went through the motions for the sake of the widow standing next to her. She walked over to the body, checked his dilated pupils and lack of pulse.

Susan Grund stood behind the technician, muttering, "Do something, do something."

"Your husband is gone, ma'am," replied Shaffer.

"No, no, give him some oxygen and some blood."

A few minutes later, Miami County Sheriff's Department Deputy Jan Kendall arrived on the scene. He immediately recognized the victim as Jimmy Grund. Kendall had known him for seventeen years.

It was just past midnight on August 4, 1992.

Meanwhile, Susan was still desperately living in hope of a miracle. "He needs blood, he needs blood, they won't help him, he needs blood."

Susan kept weeping and wringing her hands with a damp cloth.

Then she picked up the mobile phone and called her sister, Darlene. "Something is the matter with

Jim, there's blood everywhere," Susan Grund said over the phone to Darlene.

"I'll be right over."

Darlene and her husband George rapidly covered the three-mile drive over to her sister's vast home at number seven, Summit Drive, in Peru, Indiana. More police officers had already shown up on the scene.

By this time, Susan seemed numbed by what had happened. She picked up the cordless phone and called her husband's good friend Dr. John Crawshaw and tried to get him to take her husband to the hospital. When he did not answer, she grabbed a telephone directory and tried to raise Indianapolis attorney Jim Boyles, but he wasn't home, either.

E.M.T. Carolyn Shaffer then asked Susan how this tragedy had occurred and her response seemed rather puzzling.

"This place is a mess. I don't know what happened," she snapped back at the technician. Susan Grund sounded more irritated by the upturned furniture left by the intruder than by the apparent murder of her husband.

On arrival at the scene, Sgt. Bob Land of the Miami County Sheriff's Department immediately contacted the Peru post of the Indiana State Police and asked them to tell investigator Robert Brinson that an apparent homicide had occurred and the victim appeared to be wealthy local attorney and former county prosecutor Jimmy Grund.

At that precise moment, Bob Brinson was working another case of a man who had been trying to kill his wife in nearby Wabash County. He was actually at a judge's house attempting to get an arrest warrant when the call about Jimmy Grund came through. Like most folk in Peru, Brinson knew the Grunds.

The state trooper immediately told the officer accompanying him to take the warrant and go serve it, because he knew this new homicide was obviously going to take priority.

Brinson's antenna went up the moment he heard the news about Jimmy Grund because he had been called out to investigate a number of incidents at their large, imposing house in the past.

At 1:07 A.M., Jim Grund's law practice partner Don Fern got a call from Susan. "Something terrible has happened to Jimmy," she told him.

Don Fern was puzzled that Susan continually referred to her husband as "Jimmy." She had never called him that throughout their entire marriage. It was always "James," or, just occasionally, "Jim."

Don Fern spluttered out, "What?"

Then Susan's sister Darlene came on the phone and explained what had happened.

At 1:10 A.M., Indiana State Police Investigator Brinson drove into the circular drive of the property on Summit Drive in his blue Ford Taurus. Bob Brinson was troubled by other thoughts at that moment; he recalled visiting the house a couple of years back after a particularly baffling break-in. Could these two incidents be connected? He pulled up at the garage area where a number of spectators had gathered, walked through the garage, into the kitchen, and on through to the living room area where he found Susan Grund. She was sitting alongside her sister, Darlene.

Bob Brinson's first priority that night was to ensure that no one disturbed anything at the crime scene, and he intended to seal the house as quickly as possible. E.M.T. Paul Comerford immediately pointed out to Brinson that he had spotted a spent 9 mm. shell casing on the carpeted floor near the bed next to where Jimmy Grund had been shot. E.M.T. Comerford assured Brinson that the all-important shell casing had not been disturbed from its original position.

As Brinson turned towards the bedroom where the victim lay, he saw Miami County Coroner Dr. Dan Roberts arrive in his wagon outside the house. Brinson waited for the coroner and then escorted him to the ground floor bedroom. Brinson stood back as Dr. Roberts examined the body carefully before declaring that he intended to hold a full autopsy later that day at Dukes Memorial Hospital. Dr. Roberts also informed Brinson that the examination would be conducted by forensic pathologist Dr. Dean Gifford. Brinson noted all this, aware that his Indiana State Police colleague Sgt. Dean Marks would be assigned to attend the autopsy after collecting body samples and evidence from the scene.

All over Peru, news of Jim Grund's death was being relayed to the town's most important citizens with remarkable speed. County prosecutor Wilbur Siders was awoken by Kim Fenton of the sheriff's department, who told him there had been a shooting at Jimmy Grund's house. It never even dawned on Siders that his old friend and colleague Grund was the victim.

On the other side of town, Jimmy Grund's good friend Peru Police Department Sergeant Gary Nichols got a call from the Miami County Sheriff's office telling him to answer his door in about thirty seconds because "there's going to be someone there who wants to talk to you." As it happened, he had already noticed the tan and dark brown sheriff's cruiser pull up outside his house.

Nichols presumed he was about to be dragged out of bed for a search warrant. He got a nasty shock when a deputy told him that Jim Grund had been killed. The moment they told him, Gary Nichols reckoned he knew precisely who did it.

Over on Main Street, in Peru, Miami Circuit Court Judge Bruce Embrey and Gary Nichols knocked on the door of Grund's son David's apartment.

"Your father's dead," was all Embrey had to tell David Grund before he collapsed.

The whirl of the motordrive of crime scene specialist Dean Marks's camera soon echoed through the thin walls of the seven-year-old house as he took dozens of shots of the corpse and surrounding area. Later, he switched to a videocamera just to ensure nothing was missed before testing certain areas of the house and even the family car for traces of gunpowder residue. Nothing was found. In Sergeant Marks's experience it was unusual for everyone in a house where someone had been killed by a firearm *not* to have some residue on them, since the powder was kind of infectious.

Brinson then allowed Jimmy Grund's corpse to be removed by the E.M.T.s, who took it to Dukes Memorial Hospital where a detailed examination could begin. But what really concerned Brinson was the damage caused to the bedroom by the intruder. It was almost exactly the same as the damage at the break-in that had occurred at the house two years earlier.

Just as the body bag was being zipped up, Miami County Prosecutor Wil Siders arrived at the house clutching a search warrant that he already had obtained from Judge Bruce Embrey, who accompanied him. Bob Brinson gave Siders and Embrey a brief glance. He wasn't surprised the big brass had showed up so quickly because just about everyone at that scene knew Jimmy Grund personally. Grund had been the county prosecutor in the early '80s. If the same crime had occurred then, he would have expected Grund to have been one of the first on the scene. This is going to be a long night, thought Bob Brinson to himself. And it was only just beginning.

Susan Grund insisted to Bob Brinson and his state police colleagues that her husband must have disturbed a burglar. In the bedroom, investigators found two suitcases opened with their contents sprawled across the floor. Also, there was evidence that the adjoining master bedroom walk-in closet had been ransacked. In another corner of the bedroom, Susan Grund's jewelry cabinet had four drawers removed and stacked one on top of another. They also found that Jimmy Grund's dresser drawers had been opened with his clothing partially removed and piled on the floor.

Brinson continued watching Susan closely. He had experienced her idea of emotional upset two years previously during that burglary inquiry, and this time she was behaving in exactly the same way. She seemed to be crying without shedding actual tears. She still had that damp rag in her hand and kept dabbing her eyes with it.

Susan seemed extremely concerned about getting everything in the house straightened out.

Susan remained in the living room area of the house throughout all the initial police activity along with her sister, Darlene Worden and her husband, George. They were seated in one corner of the room adjacent to the master bedroom where the victim had been found shot dead.

Brinson asked Susan if she would examine the suit-

cases and the walk-in closet to determine if anything
was missing. She coolly breezed businesslike into the
bedroom and informed the investigator that there did
not appear to be anything missing from the suitcases.
Then Susan turned and walked into the closet and
told Brinson that her jewelry box definitely had been
disturbed. She noticed several rings, necklaces, and
earrings missing.

"What about your husband's belongings, Mrs.
Grund?"

Susan looked up at Brinson and then headed for his
drawers.

"Doesn't seem to be anything missing, Bob."

Brinson nodded and ground his teeth together. He
sincerely wished she would stop calling him "Bob."
After all, this was an investigation into her husband's
homicide. Sure, he'd met her a handful of occasions in
the past, but why the hell did she continue calling him
"Bob"? But for the time being he chose to ignore her,
although he called her "Mrs. Grund."

Susan went on to tell Brinson that it was entirely
possible her husband may have had some cash in his
drawers following their recent return from a vacation
in Alaska.

Then Bob Brinson found his attention captivated by
a photograph that was precariously positioned on the
top front drawer edge, complete with a belt neatly
balanced on top of it, holding it in place. It was a
seminude picture of Susan Grund and the way it was
positioned there reminded Bob of a movie set rather
than a scene of a burglary which had apparently
ended in homicide.

He looked down at the floor immediately in front
of the drawers and saw four similar photographs of
Susan Grund scattered on the floor by the dresser.

She was scantily clad and Brinson could not help noticing she had a hell of a fine figure.

Bob Brinson then escorted Susan Grund back to the living room and the comforting shoulders of her sister Darlene while he continued his examination of the murder scene. He was puzzled by the distinct lack of a forced entry and further bemused when Darlene advised him that the walk-in garage had been locked when she arrived on the scene following the call from her sister.

Brinson was also beginning to get a little irritated by Susan's demeanor. Why didn't she want to leave the house? After a murder most relatives want to get out of the house almost immediately.

While all this was going on, Darlene's husband George picked up Susan's daughter Tanelle and their own daughter Andrea and took them to Susan's mother's house three miles down the road, in the center of Peru.

Not surprisingly, the two little girls were hysterical when they arrived at their grandma's home. Tanelle kept repeating, "Daddy's dying. Daddy's dying." The two little girls hung onto George and continued sobbing uncontrollably. Susan's mother Nellie Sanders took them to her bed and cuddled them for the rest of the night.

Back at Summit Drive, Susan Grund tried once again to phone attorney Jim Boyles at around 3:00 A.M. He was a good family friend of the Grunds and this time he was in. He had some very businesslike advice for the grieving widow. He told her to inform her sister that neither of them should give any more help to the investigators.

Darlene was astounded when her sister told her what the attorney had said. What on earth did they have to hide, she wondered. Darlene turned to Bob Brinson and said she would not listen to her sister and she would be more than happy to answer any questions he had for her.

Brinson then went back to the bedroom where the murder had been committed. He was doubly irritated because there were far too many people inside and outside that house where the body had been found, including county prosecutor Siders and Judge Embrey, who were standing in the driveway. It was bad enough having a crime scene literally flooded with people, but when the victim was one of the county's most prominent citizens it just added to Brinson's burden. A lot of people were already trying to tell him how to do his job and he had no doubt it would get a whole lot worse.

In the living room area, Brinson was appalled to overhear two officers discussing their theories as to who had committed the killing. When county prosecutor Wil Siders suggested interviewing certain people there on the spot, Brinson intervened. This was his investigation and no one—however rich and powerful—was going to prevent him from doing his job in a fair-minded manner. That was the final straw; Brinson herded everyone out of the house and off the property. Some were none too happy about it, but, he explained, he had a job to do. Brinson had the unenviable task of actually proving that someone had murdered Jimmy Grund. He wanted to stay unbiased, but it was difficult in this hostile atmosphere. Certain people had already made up their own minds about the identity of the killer.

Then Bob Brinson gently advised Susan that as the investigation continued he would almost certainly have to ask her a lot more questions.

"That's no problem, Bob," purred Susan.

Brinson grimaced at the sound of her using his first name again.

"We may even ask you to take a polygraph examination," said Brinson hesitatingly.

"That's no problem either, Bob," came her reply.

Not once did she question the clear implication that police already suspected she was in some way involved in her husband's murder.

# One

Almost thirty-four years earlier, Susan Grund was
born Sue Ann Sanders in Vincennes, in southern Indiana. Not long after her birth, on October 10, 1958, the
family moved to Peru, a small town more than sixty
miles north of Indianapolis, known primarily for the
constant sound of the freight trains blowing their
horns at all times of the day and night as they shunted
across the dozens of level crossings spread through
the town.

Susan's father, William Sanders, was a serious alco-
holic whom she later claimed had sexually and physically abused her. To add to the family's problems, she
had an older brother who was retarded and died at
age thirty-two in 1981. Another brother, Eddie, died
of cancer on May 9, 1983.

When Susan was in second grade at school, her father got drunk and whipped her so hard she thought
she was going to die. She suffered an appalling burn
on the back of her left hand during the attack. The
scar is still there to this day.

By the time Susan reached twelve, she was a striking-looking brunette school girl of almost five feet six inches in height with a pretty, well-defined face and deep, dark saucerlike brown eyes. Within months of arriving at Peru High School, she was on the must-date list of almost every eligible boy in town.

Susan's mother Nellie had been born on a farm just outside Vincennes and came from a family of French settlers, who had been given five hundred acres of land near Vincennes through an incentive scheme set up in the late 1800s to encourage new settlers to move to the area.

Nellie married Susan's father William Sanders when she was just eighteen. He worked in the steel industry at the time. It was a tightly knit community, run on similar lines in many ways to the strict Amish.

Nellie was an honorable, honest mother to her children, by all accounts. Her motto in life was (and still is): *I am not going to lie 'cause lying'll get you round and get you back and get you more trouble than it's worth.*

She had seven children in all: Eddie, Rita, Randy, Darlene, Susan, Symbolene, and David. Susan always stood out because she was very pretty and possessed a determined streak that made her seem much brighter than her other brothers and sisters. She was the little princess who would one day find a rich and handsome prince and live happily ever after in a palace up on a hill. Living as part of a family who were too poor to afford anything but the most basic possessions was shaming to Susan. She was determined to do something about rectifying that one day.

Meanwhile, she had to make do with living in cramped conditions with the rest of her vast family in the most rundown house on the street where she lived.

The Sanders children all got along fairly well when they were younger. Susan was always good at helping out in the house and made a real effort to keep the place spic and span. She wanted to ensure it was a home to be proud of, if ever she invited a friend home from school. But, gradually it dawned on Susan that her scruffy home was too shaming to let her friends see so she tended to go round to other children's houses instead.

From a remarkably early age, Susan was very good at always remembering to give her mother birthday cards and Mother's Day cards. Susan also developed a virtual obsession about what clothes she would wear and she was constantly changing the color and style of her hair. She used to make an average of one new dress every week and then pretend to her school friends that her mother had bought the dress.

Susan did not get on with her father from the time he started attacking her. In later life, the very thought of what he had done to her would make her clench her fists in anger. Her voice level would rise and she would repeatedly see the images of what he did to her over and over again.

Susan ultimately became a self-destructive person following the psychological and emotional damage inflicted by her father. As a child she did not receive the sensory stimulation she required and could not establish a boundary between herself and the world beyond her tightly knit family. Even as a pretty young child she began to become an all-encompassing individual, seeing something from her own perspective and no one else's. Her brothers and sisters soon noticed how fearless Susan became and the way she would rule the

rest of the family without any sense that she hurt anyone else. Whenever Susan would do something bad,
she seemed to feel little remorse and showed little
sympathy for her "victim."

But beneath the bubbling, pretty exterior there lay
within Susan an inner sadness caused primarily by the
fact that she seemed incapable of actually enjoying
any childlike preoccupation. In reality, she never
seemed to learn how to be genuinely happy. Childhood should be a pleasurable experience in which the
developing individual learns how to be happy and de-
rive happiness from as many situations as possible.
But Susan's family and few childhood friends soon
came to the conclusion that she was not physically
capable of sensing pleasure.

Then there were the dreams that Susan experienced as a child; the continuum of reality was so often
shattered by nightmares that seemed to project such
horrific images that she found it impossible to believe
that life could be happy. All her loved ones and relatives who had died filled these dreams, but there was
one over-riding character who would keep coming
back for more—her father. Those dreams should have
been as pleasurable as they were fearful.

But Susan's sleeping fantasies had their own twisted
symbology, steeped in terror of some dreadful memories and fears that seemed to be permanently stored
in her mind. However, according to certain friends
and family, the most disturbing aspect of all this for
the young Susan was that she would sometimes find
herself in a half dreaming, half waking state that combined memories and terrors with reality of some of
her terrible experiences at the hands of her father, or
some other demonlike figure. She would find that
these dreamlike fantasies would intrude upon her life

with increasing frequency and without warning and she would often find herself in a world of her own terror-filled living nightmares with no basis for determining whether she was dreaming or waking. In these dreams, people's identities would become confused. Susan started to become more and more locked inside that dream world while the real world seemed to be filled with people without real identity and meaning.

Susan kept telling herself when she was a teenager that she would never punish her own children the way her father had hurt her. She was going to be a good, calm mother whose children would love and adore her. Unfortunately, the children of violence frequently repeat their own parent's mistakes.

Susan was fifteen when she started dating her first serious boyfriend. Chip Groat was a member of a reasonably well off local family who owned the main truckstop on the edge of Peru. Susan worked there weekends and soon ingratiated herself to Chip. Compared to her impoverished family, the Groats seemed wealthy. So, when Susan had a major bust up with her family after yet another attack by her father, she persuaded Chip's folks to let her stay at their big house on the edge of town. It was Susan's first taste of the good life. She soon became doggedly determined never to be poor like her family. She decided she would do whatever it took to make sure she had everything she wanted and needed. Her first move in that direction was to change her name from Sue Ann to Susan as it definitely had a much classier ring to it. That also meant she could distance herself from the dreadful assaults that were inflicted upon her when she was Sue Ann. Now she was Susan, she could step back and consider things from a fresh perspective.

However, life at the Groat household turned sour

for Susan when she and Chip fell out. Soon after that, she was asked to leave their spacious property. The thought of returning to her squalid home appalled Susan, so she drifted twenty miles south to the relatively larger town of Kokomo and fell in with a group of musicians, led by a handsome lead singer called Ronnie Lovell. She never once considered going back to her family. They were already becoming a part of her distant past.

The night Susan first met Ronnie Lovell, she made love to him up against a wall behind the hall where he had just performed. Her friends teased her that she had behaved more like a groupie than a respectable country girl. But Susan did not look at it like that. She was proud of her conquest of Ronnie and openly talked about every single detail of their sexual encounter.

But her friends were astonished when—just a few weeks later—Susan married Ronnie Lovell. She was aged just seventeen. Ronnie was in his midtwenties and spent most evenings working in local bars and clubs, but anything had to be better for Susan than the boredom and drudgery of life with her family back in Peru.

Ronnie's band was called Mannequin and they produced the type of heavy-metal sounds that have made groups like Aerosmith rich and famous. Ronnie moved into a cramped apartment with Susan on Washington Street, in the center of Kokomo. She worked as a hostess at the local Ponderosa Steak House and would travel with Ronnie when he played gigs at local high school dances. Sometimes, she even joined the group on stage as a backing singer.

There were occasions when Susan suspected that Ronnie was sleeping with other women. Once or twice she caught him in a clinch with a girl when she turned up unexpectedly at a gig.

Ronnie's biggest problem was that he adored himself before anyone else. He was always glancing in the mirror, combing his long, wavy brown hair. Susan started to realize that Ronnie was married to Ronnie, rather than anyone else.

This intensely irritated Susan because she kept wondering why he did not pay her more attention. Eventually, Susan got her revenge by having sex with other men when the fancy took her. *Two can play at this game,* seemed to be her motto in those days.

Ironically, Ronnie and Susan eventually moved to an apartment back in Peru, just a short distance from her family home. This bothered Susan a great deal because she had managed to escape the clutches of her father, and now she was back on the same tatty street to which she had sworn she would never return. It annoyed her a great deal to be facing a daily reminder of her poverty stricken past.

Eventually, Susan encouraged her wayward husband to move back to his hometown of Oklahoma City, where Ronnie was offered a reasonable deal to join a local group singing in bars and clubs. Susan continued to sleep with other men at this time and even lost a baby. No one ever dared ask her if she had an abortion or a miscarriage.

Once in Oklahoma City, Susan managed to persuade some of her brothers and sisters and a few friends to join her, and soon she had a collection of friends and relatives living with her in the same apartment block.

However, on the work front, things were not going so well for Ronnie. The band he had joined did not have enough gigs to support themselves full time, so he worked on construction sites by day and Susan got a job as assistant manager of the Brookwood Village apartment complex on SW 89th Street in Oklahoma City where they all lived.

Three doors down in that same block was a hand-some-looking trucker called Gary Campbell. He often hung out with Susan and her pals, particularly when Ronnie was working late. Soon, Susan and Gary started an affair.

The Christmas following their move to Oklahoma City, Susan was spotted by Ronnie coming out of Gary's apartment. Instead of confronting his wife, Ronnie asked one of her best friends if Susan was having an affair with Gary. The friend shrugged her shoulders with embarrassment.

When Susan reappeared in her own apartment a few minutes later, Ronnie angrily confronted Susan about her relationship with Campbell. She immediately started packing her things. Realizing she was leaving, Ronnie changed his tune and begged her not to go, but Susan had already organized a bed for herself in Gary Campbell's apartment.

Gary Campbell was a well-built, fair-haired twenty-four-year-old who tended to live in cowboy boots and jeans. At first, he had insisted to Susan that he did not want to get involved with her, but Susan had already decided he was going to become her next full-time man.

Susan divorced Ronnie Lovell shortly after moving in with Gary Campbell and they married in the summer of 1979. She was already pregnant with Gary's child, and on her second marriage—and she had not yet reached her twenty-first birthday.

At first, the couple's relationship seemed to have

been made in heaven. Susan was a very attentive wife, waiting on her husband, keeping an immaculately tidy home, and providing him with the best sex he had ever experienced.

But Susan could not keep up this facade of happiness for very long. Being the perfect wife was an enjoyable role for a year or so because it meant she could forget all about her troubles back in Indiana. But, as is so often the case, Campbell gradually began to fail to return the love she showered upon him and she started to nurture a deep resentment toward him. After the birth of their son Jacob, on June 12, 1979, Gary showed less and less interest in his wife.

During this period, Susan would frequently turn up back in Indiana on the doorstep of her good friend Mary Heltzel. One time, she and Mary went to a nightclub together and Susan caught the eye of a handsome man called Tim McBee and immediately began dancing with him.

Minutes later, she linked arms with McBee and waltzed out of the club into the night. Mary next saw Susan the following day when she returned to Mary's apartment having enjoyed what she described as a fantastic night of love-making. As usual, Susan was keen to share every single detail of her sexual experiences.

Back in Oklahoma City, Susan was finding husband Gary Campbell increasingly unresponsive in bed. She often spent more time alone with her fantasies instead of enjoying an active sex life with the man she had married.

Then a number of bizarre incidents occurred. One day, Gary Campbell tried to be affectionate to his wife and started to embrace Susan, an unusual move considering he had been seriously neglecting her for months. Suddenly—for absolutely no apparent reason—Susan stabbed her husband in the chest with a pair of scissors.

As blood dribbled down the front of his hairy chest, Susan started fondling Campbell. It was clear to the startled husband that his wife had got some strange, sexual kick from inflicting that injury on him. She wanted to make love to him as his wound bled all over them. Gary was appalled and pulled away. That was just the first of many sexually motivated incidents that began to make Gary Campbell wonder exactly what type of woman he had married.

Another time, Campbell informed his young wife he had injured his ankle in an accident at work and she, again for no apparent reason, stabbed him in the leg through his Levi pants with a knife. This time, Susan shouted bitterly at her husband, "Now you won't think about your ankle too much." Then, within moments of her outburst, she grabbed at his groin and started fondling him once again. Her breath was uneven and she was panting in expectation. Gary surrendered and allowed Susan to make love to him, but he was seriously concerned by what was happening between them.

Even more strangely, Susan would often go out jogging with her husband and make a point of "punching him around" as part of their fitness routine. Later at home, she would always try to hit him even harder. Gary Campbell never really fathomed whether this was because she was angry with him or sexually excited by inflicting pain. But love-making sessions after her "punch around" were usually highly charged and erotic.

During their marriage, Gary and Susan regularly went out shooting guns on ranges together. Gary was impressed by what a good shot Susan turned out to be. He used to tell her she had an evil eye. There was even one occasion when Susan shot a can in water from a bridge seventy-five feet away. Gary couldn't believe his eyes. Susan treated it as if it was an everyday occurrence.

Gary also never forgot how Susan would lose her temper sometimes when their baby cried, and then spank him ridiculously hard.

There were other more traditional moments of domestic discord like the time Gary noticed that $300 was missing from his dresser and he accused Susan of taking the cash. She denied it, but he knew she had the money.

Another time, Gary took off his family ring and put it in his toolbox and it went missing. Susan emphatically denied stealing the ring, but two years later Gary noticed Susan's father wearing exactly the same ring, during a rare get-together with her family.

In the middle of all this, Susan and Gary continued to raise baby Jacob. When they eventually split up and got a divorce after five years of marriage, Susan was given custody of the boy.

That was to be the first in a long line of unfortunate decisions made by courts of law that involved Susan.

When the first white men walked into Oklahoma in 1541 they found scattered bands of Caddo, Wichita, Pawnee, Osage, Comanche, Kiowa, Cheyenne, and Arapaho Indians. Most of them were wandering tribes who set up camp and hunted buffalo. The name Oklahoma comes from the Indian words *ukla*, "person," and *huma*, "fed."

The residents of Oklahoma remain its best resource—from the descendants of those thirty-seven

Native American tribes that call the state home to the offspring of European settlers, cowboys, outlaws, oil barons, homesteaders, coal miners, and farmers, all who came in search of the American Dream in the late 1800s.

When the move west began, people did not trickle into Oklahoma, they came in a rush—a land rush. Masses of people, wagons, and horses were lined up, a gun was fired, and they raced pell-mell to stake out the land.

Oklahoma is tallgrass prairie and everlasting mountains. Coal, gas, and oil deposits are plentiful; cotton and corn are grown in the wetter and warmer southeastern regions. Along the Oklahoma Panhandle, a dry, elevated strip extending west along the top of Texas, the High Plains terrain is suited mainly to grazing.

November 26, 1926, was the day Oklahoma became home to hundreds of miles of blue highway when the nation's first continuous stretch of paved road—linking the heartland and the west—was born. It stretched from Chicago to Santa Monica, spanning 2,400 miles, eight states, and three time zones. In the following decade, Route 66 became more than just a cross-country passage for commerce and early auto travelers. It touched lives and inspired a culture all its own. For Dust Bowl farmers (and legendary balladeer Woody Guthrie) it was the road that beckoned with the promise of boundless opportunity. John Steinbeck called the highway Mother Road in his poignant novel of the bittersweet 1930s, *The Grapes of Wrath,* a book that offers testimony to the inner strength and resiliency of the Oklahomans.

They say that if you believe adventure lies less at travel's end than in the journey itself, then Route 66 is the ideal road. Rich with history and nostalgia, the famed "Main Street of America" offers a unique glimpse into the heyday of American automobile travel. For Susan Campbell—as she was then known—it offered an opportunity to continually escape from the harsh realities of life. She seemed to be endlessly following the route of that famous road for some sense of inner peace.

Oklahoma City itself is located on the North Canadian River and has a population of around five hundred thousand. It was founded by ten thousand homesteaders on April 22, 1889, on the first day of legal settlement after they dashed across the border from Kansas to stake claims on the free land of Oklahoma. The discovery of oil in 1926 brought real prosperity to the area.

However, in the early 1980s Susan Campbell found herself trapped in Oklahoma City with her husband and child. She was bored, restless, and on the lookout for an opportunity. That opportunity could only come to her in the shape of a man. It had worked for her so far in life. Why shouldn't it continue to do so?

Gary Campbell was fairly resigned to the fact that Susan was promiscuous. So he was not exactly surprised when he heard that his pretty young wife had been having an affair with a man at the factory where she worked.

Susan was on the product line at Perry Filters Inc., one of Oklahoma City's most successful manufacturing firms, and she had managed to catch the eye of recently widowed Tom Whited. His wife had died of leukemia just six months previously, leaving him with a two-year-old son to bring up alone. Tom's deceased wife just happened to have been the daughter of the owner of Perry Filters's parent company.

Rumors of an affair between Tom and Susan were fueled by the fact that a number of Gary Campbell's relatives worked at the company and everyone, it seemed, knew about the relationship.

Gary refused to react to the stories at first because he still hoped to hold onto Susan, despite her propensity for illicit sexual liaisons. He presumed the relationship would fizzle out, but when the rumor mongers persisted, he decided to put Susan to the test about her movements. It didn't take much effort to catch her out lying and Gary rapidly concluded that his wife's affair with Whited had to be very serious. Gary even discovered that Susan was skipping her shift at work to meet Tom Whited. He must be rich, thought Gary, otherwise she wouldn't be bothering.

# Two

Susan was delighted with her latest conquest, Tom Whited. He was handsome, confident, and had a good job. He also had a nice house in one of the swishiest districts of Oklahoma City. Susan rapidly decided she had big ambitions for herself and Tom Whited, and began turning her steamy affair into a prospective marriage. Tom Whited was captivated by Susan, not least because she was so fantastic in bed. She was capable of the sort of eroticism he never even knew existed.

Tom Whited was a well-educated man. He was a graduate of Rice University and had been a captain in the U.S. Army before being discharged following an auto accident. Whited suffered a cerebral contusion in that crash and was unconscious for three weeks prior to his discharge. He resigned his commission in the army on January 10, 1981.

Before the death of Tom Whited's first wife Cheryl Ann, her father Lester Suenram promised Cheryl he would make sure his grandson Tommy was taken care of because there were fears that his father, Tom, might not be able to cope on his own.

Tom had been given a job running the wire wrack-ing company owned by his father-in-law on a sprawl-ing industrial park on the outskirts of Oklahoma City. Tom earned more than $20,000 a year. His in-laws felt a responsibility to keep him working for the sake of their grandson.

But when Tom started dating Susan at the factory, it created an almighty furor amongst his in-laws. Tom was furious about their interference and told them to mind their own business.

Father-in-law Lester Suenram insisted his only con-cern was little Tommy. Cheryl had always been so good at running the house and Tom had hardly been involved in the bringing up of the child until her ill-ness. They appreciated that Tom was having a difficult time following his wife's death, but they found it diffi-cult to deal with the blatantness of his affair with Su-san.

Tom's other problem was that he wanted to be his own man, even though he worked for his father-in-law. He resented Lester and would go out of his way not to ask advice from him. He wanted to make all his own decisions, even though they were frequently in-correct.

Lester found it extremely hard to keep calm about the situation. Susan did not seem to be the right kind of person to be marrying Tom. Lester and his family tried to convince Whited not to do it, because they had a bad feeling about Susan. There was something about her that no one trusted at the factory. They felt she was a manipulator.

But Tom would hear none of it. As far as he was concerned, he had met the girl of his dreams after all those heartbreaking months he experienced during and following Cheryl Ann's death. This was going to be the start of his new life and he was determined not to let anything get in his way.

Tom and Susan married in October 1982, in Austin, Texas, just one year after the death of Tom's first wife. But the couple's two children, Jacob and Tommy, were not taken to the ceremony. Instead, they were left behind in Oklahoma City because Susan thought their presence would ruin the enjoyment of their big day. None of Cheryl Ann's relatives were asked to the ceremony, either.

The Whited's new home on Rushing Road, in northwest Oklahoma City, was the same house bought for Tom and Cheryl by his then father-in-law Lester Suenram as a wedding gift more than six years previously. Tom bought Susan a fur coat right after their marriage as a belated wedding gift. She used to like wearing it to the shops just to annoy her neighbors. Susan seemed to settle down quickly to the life of a middle class housewife with her son Jacob and stepson Tommy. Only three months separated the ages of the boys, so she got into the habit of dressing them virtually identically. She had decided to pretend they were twins because it was much easier than explaining to other people that she and her husband had been married before.

Susan's proudest possession at that time was a photograph of the two boys both wearing identical dark blue suits with white shirts and bowties. She was forever pulling the snapshot out of her purse and proudly showing off her two boys to anyone who seemed vaguely interested.

The boys were like opposites in many ways. Tommy was the charming, bright sociable one who doted on his aunt and grandparents. He never stopped talking and had an interesting thing to say about most subjects. Many of his relatives predicted a fine future for the little boy because he seemed *so* bright.

Jacob, on the other hand, was far more withdrawn and unsociable. He appeared to be a little afraid to speak his mind. It was almost as if he had been told that old proverb, *Children should be seen and not heard.* Jacob was definitely a child who stayed firmly in the background.

But it was Tommy who clearly irritated Susan, mainly through his never-ending little boy's curiosity about things. He was always asking questions, picking up ornaments, and demanding to know what they were. Susan found him to be a complete pain and was always telling him not to touch things. She was more used to Jacob who kept silent on most things and would certainly never dare to be so impertinent.

Susan's obsession with her appearance had been gaining momentum ever since high school and by the time she married Tom Whited it had become a daily preoccupation. Each morning, she would go to the International Spa in Oklahoma City and work out. She also never missed watching Richard Simmons on television at noon and used to follow his routine to the exact step in front of the TV set in the bedroom, dressed just in a skimpy leotard. The boys were always made to join in the exercise routines. Not surprisingly, they would end up jumping and playing around, much to Susan's annoyance. She could not understand why the boys were not able to behave and respond like adults. She would often smack little Tommy for not doing his exercises properly.

One day, Susan—who had been brought up with barely any possessions whatsoever—decided that all the boys' old toys should be deposited in the garage at the house in Rushing Road to make way for all the new ones. That meant the boys had to each take a toy to the garage and Susan would only allow them to take one item at a time because she did not want toys dropped everywhere in the house.

Susan got really angry with Tommy when he sneaked back into the garage and got one of his old toys back and she found it in the hallway. She smacked Tommy on his backside. The beating went on for several minutes. The next thing she knew Tommy was screaming that he was in pain. He was lying on the floor squirming in agony. Susan looked down at the little boy contemptuously and started hitting him even harder on the head with a metal Tonka truck.

On January 27, 1983, less than four months after Susan's marriage to Tom Whited, little Tommy was admitted to Baptist Medical Center suffering from a hematoma, a swelling filled with blood in the left temporal area of his brain. X-rays revealed a fracture in the right rear portion of his skull. But doctors declined categorically to state that the injury was a result of child abuse.

There was no reason for *not* reporting the case to the police. They should have been informed. Later, it was suggested that Susan and Tom Whited were friendly with one of the doctors and he decided there was no way such an affluent couple could batter their child.

But family friend Vivian Susil was not in the least bit surprised when she heard that Tommy was in the hospital. Vivian had been to school with Tom Whited and his first wife Cheryl Ann at the Putnam City High and had also felt obliged since her death to keep an eye on the child.

Vivian looked after Tommy regularly after Cheryl Ann was diagnosed as having leukemia. When Cheryl Ann eventually died Vivian became almost like a replacement mother to the child.

Vivian saw the first sign of Tommy's fear of his stepmother, during Christmas 1982, when Vivian offered Tommy some candies. Tommy—terrified that his "mommy" might find out—told Vivian, "I don't want Mommy to be mad, I don't want Mommy to be upset."

At the hospital where he was taken following his beating, one nurse who attended Tommy after surgery was performed to release pressure from his brain asked the little boy what had happened to cause his injuries and he said, "My mommy hit me."

Vivian Susil visited Tommy a few days after his operation and she noticed Susan watching her through the glass window of the ward throughout her visit. It was as if she was keeping an eye on Tommy just to make sure he did not give any clues away as to his horrible life inside that house on Rushing Road. Vivian even put the little boy on her knee and asked him what had happened to him.

"She dropped me on my head because I wouldn't do my exercises," came the reply.

A few minutes later, Vivian tried to corner Tom about his son's allegations against Susan.

"That's crap," screamed back an angry Tom Whited.

Some days later, Vivian offered to stay at the hospital and look after Tommy while Tom and Susan went out for a break. Susan had little Tommy sitting on her lap shivering with fear as she patted him on the knee.

Vivian never forgot the blank expression of terror on his face.

One nurse was horrified when Tommy spilled a drink and the child became hysterical because he feared he would be hit by the nurse. Tommy instantly started screaming, "I'll clear it up. I'll clear it up."

Later, when Susan was asked if she ever had trouble with Tommy spilling things at home, her only response was, "Yes, Tommy is a little careless. . . . "

After a week-long stay in hospital, little Tommy was released back into the custody of Tom and Susan without any attempt to call in the police.

A few weeks later, Susan and Tom Whited decided to take a vacation in Europe. There was absolutely no question of taking either Jacob or Tommy along, even though Tommy was still not fully recovered. Vivian Susil looked after the boys.

The European trip was really a belated honeymoon for Tom and Susan. Tom had a brother in Germany, whom they visited. It was Susan's first ever trip outside the United States. She hated the long flight and could not deal with the jet-lag when the couple arrived in Europe. To make matters worse, Susan and Tom were carefully searched by customs agents on their return to the U.S. The agents' attention was caught by another fur coat Tom Whited had bought for his wife. For Susan, those two fur coats represented the beginning of her new life. It was going to be a life without poverty, a life without struggle. She was reinventing herself into a classy lady and nothing—and no one—was going to get in her way.

Even after Tommy's "accident" in January, Susan still insisted that Tommy watch and participate in the Richard Simmons TV "keep fit" sessions. Susan was still angry at Tommy because she did not know what the little boy had told the doctors at the hospital while he was being treated for those horrific injuries. This fear of being found out made her take out even more of her anger and frustration on the child.

Susan began to imagine that Tommy was doing things to get his own back on her. She convinced herself that he was not prepared to accept her as his mother. She saw his behavior as further evidence of his rejection of her. In her mind, Susan could never accept that she might be at fault. It had to be someone else.

As Susan became increasingly twisted about Tommy, every incident—however small—that occurred started to take on a hidden agenda as far as she was concerned.

The worst example revolved around the brand new Buick Riviera that Tom Whited bought his pretty young wife shortly after their marriage. That car was Susan's pride and joy. She had it cleaned every week, sometimes even twice a week, and she did not allow the children to spill a crumb on the rear seats. In fact, they were banned from ever eating or drinking anything in the vehicle.

Susan was exceptionally possessive about the Buick. She seemed to be more emotionally attached to it than to her own stepson. So, it made her very angry when Tommy urinated in the car several times after his visit to the hospital following that "accident" in January 1983.

Susan decided that Tommy was doing this deliberately. It was all part of his rejection of her as a mother, she believed. She did not once stop and consider what might be causing the boy to respond this way.

On one occasion, she made little Tommy stand in

the living room while she called Tom Whited at work
to tell him what had happened to her lovely car, her
pride and joy. Tom was then expected to tell the child
off on the phone.

Another incident happened a few weeks later when
she took Tommy and Jacob out and put them in the
car before setting off on a shopping trip. To her horror, Tommy had candy all over his face and hands. She
took him out of the car and made him stand inside the
house by the front door while she called Tom Whited
at work yet again. This time she demanded that Tom
leave work and return to the house to discipline his
son.

Susan even persuaded Tom Whited to allow her to
get a pit bull terrier puppy. She insisted the animal
would prove a fine guard dog and a playmate for the
boys.

But Tom Whited instantly took a dislike to the dog
because it was always nipping at Tommy. Susan never
disciplined the dog for doing that, although she always got angry with the animal when it did the same
to Jacob. She insisted on keeping the dog because it
got on so well with Jacob.

Susan told her husband the dog was always attacking Tommy because the boy was so timid and would
not stand up for himself against the animal.

Meanwhile the Suenrams, Tom's in-laws from his
first, tragic marriage to Cheryl Ann, were virtually
having to fight to gain any access to Tommy. It seemed
as if Tom was deliberately preventing them from seeing their own grandson. Susan was actually quietly en-
couraging the situation because she knew the
Suenrams would start questioning her about the
never-ending flurry of bruises that constantly seemed
to cover the child's body.

In February, family friend Vivian Susil became so concerned about the well-being of little Tommy that she called up Susan and asked if she could talk to the child.

Susan's reply astounded her. "Okay, but I'll have to hold the phone for him because he's got chocolate all over his hands and he's got chocolate all over my Riviera and I'm making him keep it on him 'til Tom gets home."

When Tom did finally get home that evening, the little boy ran to his father for comfort, spreading chocolate all over his suit in the process. Tom was so furious with Tommy that he punished him further.

Vivian often looked after both Tommy and Jacob for Susan. Vivian was astounded when she discovered that Tommy was starving because his stepmother had been keeping him on a strict diet.

Vivian Susil had a really bad feeling about what was happening behind the closed doors of the Whiteds' house on Rushing Road. She heard Susan talking about Tommy in such a nasty way that she later came to the conclusion that she even might have wanted to kill her stepson.

After his first "accident," little Tommy walked with a severe limp and had a horseshoe mark on his head where surgeons had made their life-saving incision. But he seemed to be all right mentally, although he became much more reserved and everyone noticed how he jumped to attention each time Susan walked in the room.

On the Easter weekend of 1983, Susan, Tom, and the two boys actually agreed to attend Sunday lunch at the Suenrams following church. Susan was more concerned with discussing how much money her sister had spent on a baby shower than on anything vaguely related to the two children under her care.

But at that lunch, Susan discovered that Lester Suenram, the father of her husband's first wife, had taken out a hefty life insurance policy on Tommy. Lester Suenram had always bitterly regretted not doing that for his tragic daughter Cheryl Ann before her illness was diagnosed.

Susan showed a great deal of interest in the details of that policy and how much money Tom would get in the event of little Tommy's death.

The Suenrams were also rather perplexed by Susan's insistence on dressing the two boys in identical outfits. But they were even more stunned when Tommy and Jacob came to lunch and they saw that Tommy's hair had been dyed brown to match his stepbrother's.

Susan's bizarre attempts to turn the boys into twins was becoming more than just an eccentric piece of parenting.

To make matters worse, Tommy still could do no right in the eyes of his stepmother. One day, Susan got so angry with the child that she pinned the two-year-old to a stake out in the backyard of the house and left him there all day in scorching eighty-five-degree heat. The boy suffered appalling burns and blisters and began being sick from the moment she took him in that evening. She then gave him a severe beating.

The following day, at 3:30 P.M. on Saturday, May 7, 1983, Tom Whited arrived home at the family's neat, comfortable detached house on Rushing Road and found Tommy, then aged two, throwing up. The doctor was called and Tommy was given a dosage of medicine to stop his sickness. He also appeared to be suffering from sunburn.

A few hours after the doctor had left, the little boy lost consciousness. As Tom Whited later put it, "I held the little man and he was as limp as a rag."

Tom and Susan then decided to take him to hospital. As they carried little Tommy to the car, Susan pleaded with her husband, "Oh my, if we go to the Baptist Hospital they'll think I've beat him again. Let's go to the South Community." But the pediatrician they had consulted before, Dr. Quillen Hughes, was not at the South Community Hospital where he worked, so the child was immediately transferred by ambulance back to the Baptist Hospital. Tommy was readmitted to the hospital in a coma. Doctors diagnosed the problem as a brain hemorrhage and general brain dysfunction.

Bruises were found on his forehead, body, arms, legs, and around the rectum, and there was also retinal hemorrhaging in his eyes. The injuries were the result of repeated blows over the course of four to seven days.

Susan had told her husband that the boy had been involved in an accident with a shopping cart while the family was out at a local supermarket. She claimed a car had hit the shopping cart while Tommy was in it. She also insisted the little boy had suffered another accident a few days earlier when he had fallen over their pet dog and hit his head on the concrete. She said the boy had cried a little and then stopped and continued playing, so she had not felt it necessary to take him to hospital.

At 9:30 P.M. that evening Detective J. M. Einhorn of the Youth Bureau of the Oklahoma City Police Department was contacted at home by worried hospital officials. His presence was urgently requested.

Einhorn had dealt with numerous child battery cases over the years and he knew what to look for. Injuries to the arms and legs below the knee were not consistent with child abuse, but above the knee and chest and around the head, "you can pretty well know something is wrong because most children hold their hands out when they fall to grab out and reach for something."

Einhorn joined the Oklahoma City Police Department in 1968 after spotting a recruitment sign as he travelled through the city while serving in the military, following a tour in Vietnam.

What sent a cold shiver up Einhorn's spine with this case was that he had a child exactly the same age as little Tommy Whited and he could not imagine why anyone would want to hurt an innocent youngster.

Just before 10:00 P.M. that same evening, J. M. Einhorn arrived at the Intensive Care Unit on the ninth floor of the hospital.

Einhorn was met by Officer T. Nelson and Nancy Agee of the hospital medical staff. All three went to Room 5, located in the southeast corner of the ICU complex. Einhorn was stunned by the sight that greeted him; there, on the bed, a child with blondish red hair was in a prone position on his back. The child was thrashing around from side to side and Einhorn could clearly see dried blood on the inside of the boy's mouth and around the teeth and lips.

As Einhorn looked closer he saw what appeared to be second degree sunburn marks on the child's chest, arms, and legs. Panning his eyes down, he then spotted a cigarette burn on the youngster's right knee. Another similar mark was near the left ankle. Bruise marks were sprinkled across the toddler's body in a blotchy pattern. The child's face was extremely red and the sunburned areas were beginning to peel. The child's legs were in a rigid position with the toes in a locked position.

Einhorn had absolutely no doubts he was dealing with an appalling case of child abuse. He picked up the boy's medical notes and read that little Tommy Whited's injuries represented, in the view of the attending doctor, a classic example of the battered child syndrome.

J. M. Einhorn immediately left the ward and went to speak to the boy's father, Tom Whited. He advised him of his Miranda rights.

Not surprisingly, Einhorn presumed at first that it was most likely the father had been the perpetrator of these awful, violent acts. But then Tom Whited calmly revealed that this was not his son's first visit to hospital.

"Back in January he had the same type of thing," explained Whited.

Einhorn was appalled. The father was saying his son had been in hospital for a similar attack before. Einhorn told Whited they would go back to those events after he had given him a detailed account of the current situation.

As Detective Einhorn talked to Tom Whited, he shook his head in astonishment. Either this man was extremely naive, or he had inflicted the injuries to his own son.

"Did you do this to Tommy?" asked Einhorn.

"Oh my God, no," replied Tom Whited before bursting into tears. "He's the only thing I have."

Einhorn decided to terminate the interview then, and made his way into Room 5 where poor, little battered Tommy Whited lay. Einhorn asked attending nurse Debbie Holstead why his legs and feet were completely rigid.

"That's normal when an injury of this nature occurs involving brain damage." Einhorn then tracked down the notes about little Tommy's previous hospitalization. Some of the remarks made by nursing staff at the time appalled him.

He immediately headed for the waiting room of the ICU where Susan Whited was sitting. She waived her Miranda rights and agreed to be questioned.

At first, Detective Einhorn found it hard to accept that this neat, attractive woman could have done such awful things to a child. His first impression of Susan was of a woman from a good, middle class home. She was well dressed in high heels and was the epitome of good taste, in an Oklahoman sort of way. Einhorn never forgot Susan's tone when he threw Tom Whited's accusations of child battery at her at the beginning of his investigation. She would always coolly reply, "I don't know what he is talking about."

She just kept repeating over and over that she did not do it. It had the desired effect at first, because Einhorn did start to wonder about her innocence.

Susan repeated the story about the shopping cart she had made to her husband. But she admitted that her stepson's worst injuries had occurred more than twenty-four hours before they finally took the child to the hospital.

Susan Whited insisted she did not hit the child regularly although she had occasionally used her hand or a belt.

Einhorn then referred to two statements made by Tommy to hospital staff in January that mentioned how "Mommy pushed me down," and "Mommy hits me when I don't do my exercises."

Susan was startled. She paused before answering. "Well, when he doesn't do his exercises I don't hit him, I just sort of push him or tap him for him to go on."

J. M. Einhorn was deeply disturbed by what he was hearing. Here was a mother who forced her two-year-old stepson to do aerobics.

"Did you in fact push Tommy's head down to cause that injury to the front of his head?" asked Einhorn quietly but firmly.

"No." She hesitated, then went on, "Why are you accusing me?"

Just then, Susan got up to get a cup of water. Seconds later, she fainted and fell to the ground. A charge nurse immediately went to her assistance and told Susan to "wake up." She opened her eyes and said, "What happened?" The charge nurse turned to J. M. Einhorn and said, "She's faking. If she was unconscious due to the fainting she would not have woken up that quickly." It also emerged that she had "fainted" once already since bringing in little Tommy earlier that day.

While all this was happening, Einhorn decided to try and have a quick word with Susan's son Jacob, who was in a nearby waiting room with one of Susan's relatives. Einhorn offered the boy some candies and then asked the youngster how his brother got hurt.

"I don't know, but he gets hurt in the garage," came the child's instant reply.

"Does Mommy hit Tommy in the garage?"

"Sometimes he falls down."

"Are you sure?"

"Well, only when he doesn't do his exercises."

A few minutes later, Einhorn returned to Susan and asked her about the boy's claims.

"He made up the story because he heard it from Tommy," insisted Susan. Einhorn noted that she was not dry mouthed and she had looked him right in the eye. He knew that when people lie to policemen they usually fail on both counts.

That evening, Tom Whited refused to allow Susan to go back to the family home and she was eventually collected by her sister, Darlene Sanders. Understandably agitated, Whited made undisguised threats to kill his wife after realizing she had probably inflicted those injuries. But what really concerned Det. J. M. Einhorn was the fact that Tom Whited had apparently done nothing to prevent this tragedy. How could he not have known what was going on?

It was four in the morning before the hard-working detective finally left the hospital. He was determined to find out exactly how those injuries had been inflicted. It could so easily have been his child lying there helpless with tubes providing his only lifeline. It was the very least that little Tommy deserved.

# Three

When Tom Whited's first wife's sister Paddy turned up at the Baptist Hospital in Oklahoma City to see little Tommy she was horrified. Eight-and-a-half months pregnant with her second child, Paddy could barely hold back the tears when she saw what had happened to her nephew.

Tom and Susan were at the hospital, but kept a low profile throughout Paddy's visit. She did not even see them.

Detective J.M. Einhorn was very concerned about many aspects of this disturbing case, not least of all the reason why the Baptist Hospital did not call in the police following the original attack on little Tommy in January 1983.

When he interviewed Dr. Richard Crook, an old family friend of Tom's and E.R. member at the Baptist Hospital, he began to realize why. The doctor told Einhorn he thought social workers had been called in. But he also conceded that he had never accepted that such an apparently responsible couple could commit a heinous act of violence on a child.

Einhorn also discovered that Susan seemed to have an apparent compulsion to make Tommy behave in an absolutely perfect manner. She had become completely obsessed over his behavior, and that had probably contributed to his injuries.

On May 11, 1983, Det. Einhorn attended a medical examination of little Tommy by Dr. John Stuemke, chief of Pediatrics at the Oklahoma Children's Memorial Hospital. His conclusion was heartbreaking: "This youngster has to be miserable. He must have been in a great deal of discomfort. This is a battered child. There is no doubt or question in my mind whatsoever."

Besides the injuries to his brain, the doctor went on to confirm bruises and other marks over much of the little boy's body, plus those three cigarette burns to his legs.

A few days after complicated surgery had been performed to relieve the pressure on Tommy's brain, nurses tried to get him to pass water because he had been wetting his bed two or three times a day. But Tommy seemed terrified to go to the toilet. It was obvious that he had been severely punished in the past for daring to go. Every time a nurse tried to persuade him, he would go into a spasm of fear.

Meanwhile, Susan's previous husband Gary Campbell heard of what had happened and immediately applied for and got sole custody of little Jacob. Although Jacob was fairly spoiled and well looked after compared with his stepbrother Tommy, the mental scars that he suffered as a result of watching his mother inflict those dreadful punishments were horrendous.

But perhaps the most extraordinary aspect of the case was that Susan—already fast becoming the master manipulator—almost managed to convince Tom Whited that Tommy's beatings had all been a dreadful accident. She even reconciled with Tom briefly *after* the child's near-death beating. But finally, Tom Whited applied for divorce from Susan on May 18, 1983.

On May 27, 1983, Tom was forced to submit a legally binding letter to Oklahoma Assistant District Attorney Becky McNeese, promising that he would work with the Department of Human Services to help in the prosecution of his wife. Tom Whited rightly was wracked with guilt. He should have known what was happening to his son and he should have protected him from that abuse.

In the hospital little Tommy lay close to death. The mental—as well as the physical—scars were plainly obvious. It was clear the child would never recover.

However, Susan was living in a fantasy world in which she simply told herself that none of this was happening. It was all his fault; that little boy was doing it to himself by behaving so badly. Susan had become virtually an observer of her own crimes. She felt completely unconnected to the beatings suffered by her stepson and it had helped her to continue assaulting him without fearing the consequences.

Throughout Tommy's hospitalization, Susan had become much calmer and more gentle back at the family home on Rushing Road. The little boy's absence meant she could keep the home even more immaculately clean. She proudly boasted about the remodeling of the property to visitors to the house, about the new carpet and the spanking new kitchen. Tommy rarely got a mention. Susan had few material things as a child. Now, as an adult, they meant more to her than people. People were only good for one thing—betrayal; because that was all people had ever done to her.

But as soon as Tom Whited fully realized what his wife was suspected of doing to his son Tommy, he took away her checkbook, credit cards, and her car and threw her out of the house on Rushing Road. But none of that was going to make Tommy get better. He was beyond a cure. Ninety percent of his life had been beaten out of him forever.

Oklahoma City Assistant D.A. Don Deason was far from satisfied about Tom Whited's role in the case. He wondered why Whited seemed so hesitant when he talked about the situation and he never once looked Deason in the eye throughout many hours of questioning. Deason found him to be evasive in the way he answered questions. It was also really hard to keep Whited on one track at times.

Don Deason was a young, handsome lawman who had worked at the Oklahoma City District Attorney's office since graduating from the University of Oklahoma College of Law in May 1979. Deason's hobbies were running and bicycling. Every lunch time, he would run five miles at the local YMCA. On his desk at the D.A.'s vast offices in downtown Oklahoma City was a small painted wooden vulture. It was the mascot of the Oklahoma City Police Department's Homicide Division. They gave Deason the mascot as they believed he was "one of them," a prosecutor with a cop's heart.

Don Deason was particularly confused by Tom Whited's academic background—it did not fit into the regular pattern of child battery. Here was a college-educated guy with a secure, well-paying job, a nice home and yet he had allowed all this misery to be inflicted in his own house. Tom Whited was just not the sort of low lifer one usually came across in such cases, thought Deason.

Deason then examined the case against Susan. Once he had scraped away the veneer of respectability that had so impressed Detective Einhorn initially, he uncovered someone whose background qualified her as the most likely suspect. She was the one with the trailer-trash mentality and the unhappy family. Hints that she herself had been abused as a child simply reaffirmed Deason's worse fears.

In the middle of the police investigation, Tom and Susan met up to discuss the final closing down of their marriage. Out of the blue, Susan mentioned the possibility of suicide. Tom was stunned. The last thing he expected his wife to consider was taking her own life—it just was not in character with the rest of her persona.

But Susan persisted and kept bringing the conversation back to the subject of suicide. Then she asked Tom how much life insurance *he* had. At first, he did not take in the implications of what she was saying. Then it dawned on him that she was suggesting that perhaps he should take his own life. Tom never forgot the shiver that went up his spine at that very moment. He then realized that Susan was capable of doing anything to get what she wanted.

Assistant District Attorney Deason was growing increasingly disturbed by the continual contact between Susan and Tom. He could not understand why Whited kept being lured back by Susan despite the horrific injuries she had inflicted on little Tommy. It particularly bothered Deason because Tom Whited was going to be his main witness against Susan and if Tom started watering down his testimony then Deason might not ever succeed in prosecuting her. In Don Deason's opinion, that was almost as much of a crime as the beatings received by that innocent child.

Tommy was released from hospital in July 1983. He had a tracheotomy and was moved to a relative's house. He still needed oxygen and his trach had to be sectioned and cleaned regularly. He required very specialized nursing care.

Tom Whited occasionally visited his son and he continued working for his former father-in-law, Lester Suenram, even following Susan's arrest. Lester felt bitter, angry, and extremely frustrated by all the circumstances which had combined so tragically to end his grandson's normal life. These factors were:

1. How could Tom Whited have fallen in love and married such an evil woman?
2. How could Tom Whited have failed to notice what was happening in the house?
3. Why did the Baptist Hospital not report the first beating injuries to the police? If they had done so, Susan would not have been allowed near Tommy again and the second set of injuries would never have occurred.

Lester Suenram blamed himself in many ways. He felt he should have been stronger with Tom from the outset. But how on earth could any person have predicted the awful crimes that were committed against his grandson? From the day of little Tommy's release, Lester devoted his entire life to making sure his beaten and battered grandson was given all the loving care and attention he should have had from the day he was born.

On November 14, 1983, Susan appeared in court in Oklahoma City.

She was dressed as if she was on her way to attend a civic function with a carefully coordinated gray suit and modest two-inch pumps, complete with a matching gray hat. The hat certainly made her stand out from the other defendants that day. It was a circular, grand hat turned at an angle on her head.

Susan was the ultimate head-turner in court that day. Even the attorneys could not keep their eyes off her as she clipped into the art deco courtroom with its ornate ceilings and overhead gallery. Her dress conveniently matched the grey walls of the courtroom with its severe wooden pews, two square tables, a blackboard, and an ornate wooden carving showing three Indians making a peace offering. The Oklahoma state flag hung above the judge, a field of sky blue, an Indian warrior's rawhide shield bearing six painted red crosses, and dangling seven eagle feathers, and superimposed on it a peace pipe crossed with an olive branch. Below it, in white, the legend "Oklahoma."

The assembled attorneys had already made a preagreed plea, specifically designed to get the hearing finished quickly. It also conveniently helped Susan avoid having to listen to many of the gory details of the injuries which she had inflicted so cruelly on her stepson. Perhaps, if she had been made to face up to her crimes then she might have changed her ways.

The judge then asked in open court whether this agreed plea would be fair to the people of Oklahoma County. Assistant D.A. Don Deason's first thoughts were that it was not at all fair because he knew that her plea would probably mean she would not get a custodial sentence. He did not like what he was doing. He felt the case had been compromised and he has never stopped blaming himself ever since. However, Deason did not object in court that day.

But then he had no choice. There was no real additional evidence from Tom Whited and it seemed as if Susan still exerted control over him despite the fact that their divorce was under way. Deason actually believed that Susan was still sleeping with Whited up until the trial. He remained appalled by that situation because he could not understand how anyone could go back to someone who had done that to his child.

The judge then repeated his question to Deason about whether this was fair to the people of Oklahoma County.

"Yes, your honor," replied Deason, but in his heart of hearts he knew that was not the case.

The judge gave Susan a five-year suspended sentence after she pleaded guilty to child beating, a felony.

After those court proceedings in 1983, Tommy was officially declared a deprived child and placed into the custody of his maternal grandparents. Susan and Tom Whited both had their rights to the child terminated.

Perhaps surprisingly, the case was not given any space in the *Oklahoma City Times*. But then that might just have been indicative of the vast number of similar child abuse cases that come before courts across the country every day of the year. In fact, the only reference to the Whited case was in a list of felonies which stated simply, "Sue Ann Whited, 24, address unlisted, child beating."

After the trial, little Tommy's grandfather Lester Suenram fought to get full parental rights over Tommy because it was clear that no one else genuinely cared as much for the little boy. The Suenrams were outraged that Susan had been given a suspended sentence. They had seen their beloved grandchild beaten and battered to the point of no return, yet she had walked free from the courtroom.

Family friend Vivian Susil, who had looked after Tommy so often, was so upset and angry about what happened to him that she took out an album of photos of Tom, Tommy, Susan, and Jacob and cut around each photo, removing Susan and Jacob from her life forever.

The case has continued to haunt Assistant D.A. Don Deason. He felt the situation was softened by Tom Whited, who had backed down from his original damning testimony by the time the case got to court. Whited seemed to have become yet another manipulated soul in the life of Susan and he left the court that day a very sad man.

Deason recognized in Susan someone who had developed her own glamorous persona. He believed she picked Oklahoma to live in partly because it was a place with no ties to her past. It is much easier to reinvent yourself in new territory. Deason had found Tom Whited "kinda squirrely" and refused not to lay some of the blame at his door. He was especially surprised to discover that Susan had got pregnant by Whited *after* Tommy's hospitalization.

About ten days after the case finished, Deason got a call late one afternoon from Susan. Why on earth would she contact him, especially after the case had finished, he wondered.

Don Deason was very suspicious, but he took the call mainly out of curiosity. Susan got right to the point.

"There are some questions I need to ask you.

Would you meet me for a drink after work?" she purred.

Deason was astounded. The woman who had almost battered her own stepson to death was now flirting with him on the phone and asking for a date!

He laughed.

"That wouldn't be a very good idea, would it?"

Susan sighed, "Oh well . . . "

Deason put the phone down, convinced he had just avoided a very dangerous situation. He could visualize himself later that evening in some sleazy motel room when the door is kicked open and a camera pops as he tries to cover himself up. That woman is capable of anything, thought Deason to himself. Absolutely anything.

Susan was annoyed at her failure to lure Don Deason out. He would have been a handsome catch. She had this thing about lawyers. The power, the money, the glamor. It all seemed so appealing. He would have been her ticket out of that life and into the next. Oh well, she'd have to spread her web until she found herself another perfect partner.

Meanwhile, poor little Tommy was left with severe sight impairment and permanent brain damage.

"She is undoubtedly responsible for the condition that little boy is in," recalled Don Deason years later. "It's one of the most pathetic cases I've dealt with since I've been assistant district attorney."

Susan was pregnant, homeless, and penniless. There was only one place to go—home to Peru, county seat of Miami County, Indiana.

# Four

Miami County, Indiana, is just thirty miles long and twelve miles wide and covers an area of 384 square miles, about sixty miles north of Indianapolis. The county arose from the ashes of the Miami Indians following the treaty of 1763 that allowed the Native Americans the right to settle in the woodland regions along the upper Wabash and Mississinewa river valleys. Less than thirty years later, the Miamis won one of the greatest Indian victories of all time when they defeated General St. Clair and his American forces in a battle near Fort Recovery, Ohio.

White settlers reached the area in the late 1820s. And with the building of the Wabash and Erie Canal in 1832 and the first railroad in 1854, the town of Peru grew out of the deserted flatlands.

Around this time, Ben E. Wallace began a long tradition of the town's links to the circus when he purchased the C.W. Coup Circus. Eventually circuses from all over the country used the town as a staging post for their winter break.

The coming of the railroad to Miami County scattered towns around the countryside like cinders from the engines' smokestacks. Whole communities sprang up and flourished along the routes of the main railroads, only to be abandoned if the rail companies diverted away from their original boundaries.

Composer and songwriter Cole Porter was born in Peru on June 9, 1891. Cole learned to play the piano and violin before the age of six and published his first song at the age of thirteen. He died on October 15, 1964, and is buried beside his wife Linda at Mount Hope Cemetery in the middle of town.

By the turn of the century, the county seat of Peru was on its way to becoming a civilized community. Streets were paved with brick, sewer lines laid, telephone wires strung, trolleys running, and roaming geese removed to the surrounding countryside.

It's both appropriate and a bit misleading that Miami County should have been named after the once powerful Indian tribe that lived there and through much of America's midsection.

The name is appropriate because in the dawn of America's recorded history they were the territorial landlords, exercising full "ownership" prerogatives and leaving to the settlers who followed a vast and generally euphonious glossary of place names.

But the name is a bit misleading, too, for the Miamis were in fact merely caretakers in this land. They settled in the area only for a relatively brief time, going from being lords of the forest to herding cattle in just one generation. By 1840, they had virtually all gone.

In a similar sort of fashion, the family of Susan Sanders had laid claim to Peru as their home town a hundred years later. But in fact, most of her mother and father's family came from Vincennes, another Indiana settlement some two hundred miles to the south west of Peru.

The town of Peru is itself an insular community, little things can come to mean a lot. Although not that far from the state capital of Indianapolis, Peru remains the epitome of a small, rural town, a place where people are born, raised, married, and buried within the same ten-square-mile area. People know each other here. The neighbors down the street are likely to be the folk you knew in grade school, or at least in Sunday school. The people who work together also play together and pray together.

In the late spring of 1984, Susan drove back into Peru in some style thanks to her gleaming Buick Riviera, which she had managed to persuade Tom Whited to give to her, despite the battering of little Tommy.

Once in Peru, Susan quickly managed to find herself a boyfriend. His name was Rick Cook and he lived opposite her mother's home—still on the wrong side of the tracks—on 3rd Street. Susan was not particularly happy dating a poor man, but at least Rick was young and handsome and very good in bed.

However, Susan continued keeping an eye out for a more suitable long-term partner. She looked up an old friend, hairdresser George Myers, and bemoaned the fact that there were no really rich, eligible men in Peru. Then Myers came up with an idea. He was close friends with local police detective Gary Nichols, whose best friend was a recently divorced lawyer called Jimmy Grund. Susan's ears pricked up at the sound of his name. The Grunds were a legend in Peru and she would give anything to become part of that family. A few days later, Myers got Grund's close friend Nichols to arrange for Susan to go on a blind

date with Jimmy Grund. Susan was delighted. Things
were definitely looking up. She had absolutely no idea
that Nichols and Myers believed they were pulling a
massive stunt on their friend because he did not realize she was heavily pregnant.

Jimmy Grund was part of a very rich and powerful
dynasty in Peru. Grund came from a family steeped in
local law. His father was James A. Grund, a fervent
Republican who worked as Miami County Prosecutor
throughout much of the 1970s. Before that, he served
eight years as a Peru city judge. He had been a working attorney since 1950 in Peru.
    James A. Grund served with the Air Transport
Command from 1941 to 1945 and was in the China-
Burma-India theater until nearly a year after the end
of World War II.
    Jim Grund was born in Peru on December 23, 1944,
when his father was still serving in the Far East. Little
Jimmy did not even meet his father until almost a
year later when he returned home from his wartime
travels.
    Jim's mother Connie—also born and bred in Peru
and married to James A. Grund for more than fifty
years— reckoned Jim and his brother Jeff switched
personalities when Jim was about fifteen years old.
Up until then, Jim had been the calm, serious one.
But one New Year's Eve the family was sitting around
a dinner table making resolutions and Jim announced
he was "going to get out and have more fun." From
that moment on, he never looked back. Jeff, meanwhile, switched into serious work mode and has remained that way ever since.
    Jim graduated from Peru High School in 1962. One
of his teachers later reckoned that he was the bright-

est student she ever taught even though he never got straight As. His friends and family genuinely believed he did not want to be a straight-A honor kid. Jimmy graduated from Indiana University with a bachelor's degree in 1966 and went on to complete law school at IU in 1970.

Jim's father, James A. Grund, was even admitted to the bar association of the nation's highest court, the Supreme Court. He was one of only twenty-two Indiana prosecutors accepted. His new stature meant that Grund, senior, could argue appeals through courts from the county all the way to the Supreme Court.

In 1971, Jim Grund was sworn in as the then-youngest-ever member of the Miami County Bar Association. He then practised law as deputy county prosecutor from 1971–78 while his father was prosecutor. At that time, he even wrote a book on business law. The younger Grund then succeeded his father as prosecutor, serving from 1978–82. After that, father and son shared a law office on East Main Street, just a few blocks from the house where Jimmy Grund grew up.

Jim Grund was a fiery and able prosecutor by all accounts. He did not suffer fools gladly and he fast gained a reputation as a hard man in the courtroom. As prosecutor, fellow lawyers used to say that the H of his middle name stood for heartless.

Outside the court, Jim was known as a bright, sociable man who liked to fly planes and attend basketball and football games at his alma mater, Indiana University. He owned his own plane and often would joke about how he preferred flying to practising law.

Jim met his first wife, Jane, when they were at Indiana University together. His fraternity work in student registration enabled him and his pals to stop freshmen girls and get their names and date them. Jim ended up having a double date with his best pal and two girls. One of them was a pretty petite brunette called Jane Snyder. Jim, driving a 1962 Chevy complete with manual gear shift, was much in demand. Jane was eighteen and her new date just nine months older.

The couple married in January 1965—when they were both just twenty years old—and lived together in university housing. Their daughter Jama was born on July 17 that year. By this time, Jim was working full time and still going to law school, in order to support his young family.

In those days, Jim was doing very well in his day job as a production manager for RCA and he seriously contemplated taking it up as a proper career, but the lure of the legal profession was proving too strong. In any case, he also had a family tradition to uphold.

The couple's second child, David, was born on June 30, 1970, just after Jim had finished law school and was preparing for his bar exam. He had continued to support his entire family throughout all this.

Once qualified, Jim and his family moved to his grandparent's spare house on West 6th Street in Peru. But Jane was determined not to be just another homemaker and, armed with her degree in sociology, she also got herself a real estate licence so she would have two prospective careers to fall back upon when the children got older.

Daughter Jama attended Peru High School until her freshman year when she moved to the very exclusive and extremely academic Culvert Military Academy for girls. She boarded at the school, but came home most weekends.

Jimmy and Jane then started to drift apart, primarily because they had done too much too fast as a couple and the sparkle had fallen out of their relationship. However, the couple's separation came completely out of the blue as far as their friends were concerned and they agreed to divorce by mutual consent in December 1980. But the couple decided to appear to continue to live together so as to make the split less painful for their children, so both stayed on in the house. There were no other parties involved, although for the first few years following the divorce, Jane had genuinely wanted Jim to agree to remarry her.

Friends of the couple remained completely bemused by the parting. Jim and Jane had seemed to be such a perfect match. They flew light planes together. They both adored all water sports. In fact, they seemed to have more in common with each other than couples who have been married for a lifetime.

But there was another side to Jimmy Grund. It was almost as if he refused to accept that he was married and had to settle down. He loved the company of a vodka and tonic and a pretty girl, in that order.

There were also the nonstop practical jokes that Jimmy constantly used to hide his true emotions. One time, he filled a horse trough with hot water and turned it into an open air hot tub for anyone who wanted to join him. Another time, he bombed his fellow lawyer Don Fern's backyard with oranges dropped from his own plane as he swooped overhead. The idea had been to get them all in Don's pool, but most of them ended up going through the windshields of cars, as well as killing a lot of the grass in Don's backyard.

The end of Jim Grund and Jane's marriage was a very low-key event. He never even told his closest friends he had got a divorce until the day before it was made final.

Jim had a reputation as a bit of tightwad when it came to money. He used to pride himself on getting a reduced club rate at most hotels whenever he went off on a trip or a vacation. He would not give his son David any allowance money, only support money that he and Jane had agreed to in their divorce settlement.

Jane and Jim managed to get along okay after the divorce. Jim continued to be concerned about David's education and he agreed to pay half of his eventual law education expenses. Jim talked enthusiastically about having David one day join his law practice following his graduation. Jim had even taken David to Indiana University's founders' day event.

A few months before Susan went out on that first blind date with Jimmy Grund, he asked his ex-wife Jane to move out of their house. Their son David was thirteen years old at the time and struggling in eighth grade. Jane accepted the situation and found herself a comfortable rented apartment at 167 East Main Street, in the center of Peru.

Jimmy had another girlfriend at the time who was getting pretty serious about him and Jim's wife Jane presumed that was why he had asked her to move out of the family house.

Jimmy Grund was a unique combination. He was a pillar of the establishment, but he also part-owned a lively local bar. He was a man who was always going to have fun. He was forever taking macho fishing trips with his pals to far-off destinations like Canada or Mexico, flying around the country in his private plane, and enjoying more than his fair share of his favorite tipple, vodka and tonic.

\* \* \*

Just before Jimmy and Susan's blind date, word got around the lawyers and cops' favorite watering hole, Shanty Malone's bar, that Susan was a stunning-looking woman. Jim was delighted to hear the rumors although no one even hinted at the fact that she was eight months pregnant!

Jimmy Grund handled that first date with Susan like a true gentleman. The fact that she was about to have another man's baby did not seem to bother him in the slightest. The couple got on incredibly well. Jim was captivated by Susan's good looks. She even managed to make being pregnant look graceful, but then Susan had been especially careful not to let the pregnancy affect her ability to look sexy. With her light frame and slim build she actually managed to appear as if she was carrying a pea in a pod rather than a healthy, bouncing baby.

Jim's good friend Sgt. Gary Nichols was delighted that he had persuaded Grund to go on the blind date because it meant sweet revenge for a wisecrack Jim had pulled on him when he got Gary's ex-wife to jump out of his thirtieth birthday cake at a party in Shanty Malone's. Jimmy Grund had also managed to layer his friend's bed with shaving cream as an added birthday bonus when he got home that night. That was the sort of guy Jimmy was.

Gary was a tad annoyed about that—not to mention the fact that he had always harbored a vague suspicion that Jimmy had a soft spot for his then wife.

What Gary Nichols did not realize was that his payback practical joke was about to turn into a very serious romance for Jim and Susan.

In many ways, Gary and Susan were quite similar to each other, street smart, charming, shrewd, charismatic. They spoke the same language and that helped Gary rapidly see through Susan's facade.

During the early days of Jim Grund's romance with Susan, Gary even felt a twinge of jealousy. After all, Susan was a very attractive woman and Gary never actually intended to hand her on a plate to Jim Grund. His practical joke had seriously misfired and he had provided his old pal with what appeared to be a classy lady.

But the similarities between Susan and Gary Nichols would ultimately contribute to her downfall because the savvy police officer soon started to spot things about Susan that made him feel very uncomfortable in her presence. Much sooner than anyone else, he started to question her motives for falling in love with Jimmy Grund.

However, at the beginning of the relationship, Susan was just delighted to have found a safe, secure, prestigious man. Never in her twenty-five years of life had Susan met anyone like Jimmy Grund. He was mature, charming, intelligent, polite, smiling, well-groomed, educated, ambitious.

On that first date, Jim took charge and she immediately liked him, even perhaps loved him. He was direct and forceful, a man who knew what he wanted and went out and got it. She had dated so much riffraff before, perhaps with the exception of Tom Whited. Jim Grund was thirty-nine years old, hair thinning, pale complexion, slightly overweight, dressed conservatively. In some ways he reminded Susan of the way she wished her father had been.

Jim and Susan spent hours on that first date chatting away over a candle-lit meal. The two of them seemed to instantly recognize that something special was happening between them. Susan was entranced by his tales of derring-do, like scuba diving in the Caribbean and flying his plane all over the continent. She felt a twinge of sorrow for him when he recounted the end of his marriage to Jane, but she was careful not to give away too many details about her three previous marriages. Susan did not smoke, drink alcohol, or do drugs, things that Jim Grund feared might create problems for a man in such a high-visibility career. Meanwhile, his courtly manners and soft accent told Susan that she had at last found a man of which she could be truly proud.

# Five

"Darlene, what am I going to do?" Susan asked her older sister a few weeks after meeting Jimmy Grund on that blind date. "Both of them want to marry me."

Susan was referring to her handsome young stud Rick Cook and that older, more secure, but prematurely balding Jimmy Grund.

"But which one d'you love, Susan?" replied Darlene.

"I love Rick, but I don't want to be poor. What would you do?"

"I'd marry for love, Susan."

"But I don't wanna be poor, so I'm going to marry James."

Darlene wasn't that shocked by her sister's proclamation. It was typical of Susan. . . .

Darlene first met her sister's future husband when they all attended a Thanksgiving party in November 1984. Susan seemed rather tense throughout the evening while Jim was knocking back drinks at a solid rate and getting into the swing of the party. He impressed Darlene because he never once appeared uncomfortable or out of place amongst Susan's hillbilly-type relatives, many of whom lived in trailers scattered all over Indiana.

Everyone at the party had been rather hesitant about inviting Susan and her new boyfriend because Jim Grund was a pro-tem judge. And to make matters worse, some of the Sanders kids had been prosecuted by Jimmy in court over the previous couple of years.

But Grund did not bat an eyelid and he even ended up having a giggle with Darlene when he and Susan walked into a room where her sister was changing dresses and caught her stark naked. Jimmy just grinned and moved out of the room. Susan was furious. She did not want this side of her family to be revealed to the rich and powerful man she intended to make her fourth husband.

Darlene and her mother Nellie were most taken by Jim Grund. He was the kind of guy who was happy to sip a beer and sit on the porch and talk about life with whoever happened to be around. He was not a snob. He was not trying to be somebody else and he was always extremely good to Susan's family.

In 1985, he even helped Darlene purchase the house opposite her mother's on East 3rd Street. It had been owned by Susan's previous boyfriend Rick Cook, but then he fell behind on his payments and the property was virtually given away for a bargain $25,900. Darlene and her husband did not have the $5,000 deposit required but Jim went down and talked to the bank and got them the loan anyhow.

Jim Grund first introduced his own family to Susan when he took her round to his parents' detached house on Main Street and announced his girlfriend was pregnant.

Connie and James went quiet for a few seconds, trying to digest what their son had just told them.

"Er, congratulations, Jim," said his mother hesitatingly.

Then a big smile came to Jimmy's face. "Don't worry, Mom. It's not mine."

It was a hell of a way to break the ice, but then that was typical of Jimmy Grund.

A few weeks after Thanksgiving 1984, Jim Grund played the role of doting father and rushed to the hospital in Logansport with Susan as she started labor. When baby Tanelle was born, Jim was as pleased as if she were his own daughter. He looked on Susan and her newborn baby as a golden opportunity for him to make amends for not always being the best father in the world to his two eldest children, Jama and David. This time around he was going to be there when they needed him, not always off chasing down the best cases.

Susan went to great lengths to explain to Jim's family that her other child, Jacob, was currently living with her previous husband Gary Campbell whom, she said, needed his son badly because he was a virtual invalid following a motorcycle crash. She never once hinted at the horrific injuries she had inflicted on her stepson, Tommy.

When Susan's baby Tanelle was just six weeks old, Jimmy announced to his parents that he and Susan and the baby were off to Florida for a vacation.

A few days after departing on their Florida trip, Jimmy phoned his mother, Connie, back in Peru. She thought he was calling to see if his sister Jane had had the baby she was expecting. But Jim had something else on his mind.

"Are you sitting down, Mom? I have something to tell you."

Connie mumbled a "yes."

"Susan and I got married. . . ."

Connie grimaced on the other end of the line and then typically, played it all down.

"I thought that was what you were going to say, Jim."

"You gotta be shitting me, Mom?"

"Nope. I knew you'd go and do that."

Jim and his good friend Gary Nichols had made a wager that the first one of them to get remarried would owe the other $1,000. When Gary heard the news he promised himself he would get the money off Jim the moment he was back from Florida, before he had a chance to wriggle out of it.

By all accounts, Jim and Susan's wedding could not have been more romantic. They married on December 6, 1984, on a boat owned by Jim's good friend Jack Vetter, as it bobbed about on the Atlantic Ocean just a few miles off Flagler Beach. Vetter even acted as witness. Susan looked radiant in a pastel-colored dress and huge, hooped earrings. Jim Grund was immaculately turned out in a beige, lightweight suit and baby Tanelle was barely able to stay awake when a friend took a photograph of the newly married couple.

On the way back from Florida, Jim and his new wife and her baby daughter stopped off at his own daughter Jama's home in North Carolina to introduce her to Susan. Everyone seemed to get on fine. The Grunds found Susan charming enough, but they did wonder a little about her background. She talked with

a soft Sou...
tist. She nev...
raised in Pe...
were many gre...
ment the family...
himself a partner...
inely in love.

Jim Grund had jus...
for Miami County wh...
prosecutor. They were t... ...and-
son legal team in the co... ... that, she
liked that very much indee...

Once back from the weddi... Florida, Jimmy was
quickly tracked down by his buddy Gary Nichols who
demanded that check for $1,000. Nichols cashed it
immediately and bought everyone in Shanty Malone's
a drink to celebrate. What had started as the blind
date from hell had ended in marriage and a $1,000
check for Gary Nichols.

The one mystery about the entire romance had
been what became of the woman who was Jim's girlfriend at the time he met Susan. The woman had been
unceremoniously dumped and left town almost immediately. Friends said she was heartbroken, but Jim was
under the influence of a highly ambitious woman now,
someone who was determined to get to a position of
power and influence in a town where she was once
considered to be a distinctly trashy resident.

Susan was bubbling with excitement when she arrived back in Peru following the marriage, ready to
restart her life as the model wife and mother. As a
child she enjoyed being right in the thick of things and
she was determined to make sure she got treated just
as well as Jim Grund in the community. She might
even have also been head over heels in love with

...mly had no doubt he was
...elt pretty good.

...mpletely smitten by Susan. But he
...ely ambitious about his work as the
...st sought after lawyer following his four
...tint as county prosecutor. Jim would spend long,
...ong days and nights in the vast set of offices on Main
Street, where he operated his law firm.

He charmed his fellow attorneys in the practice as
well as every member of the predominantly female
clerical staff and he totally immersed himself in the
business.

At first, the happy couple and newborn baby settled
into the same house on West 6th Street where he had
brought up his first family. It was a neat, spacious
three-bedroom property but Susan was far from satisfied. She had expected Jim Grund to be living in much
more lavish style and she was determined to make
sure that they moved somewhere more in fitting with
her new status as the wife of one of the most influential men in Miami County.

A few months after his marriage to Susan, Jim
Grund went off on one of his regular fishing trips with
some of his pals, leaving Susan to her own devices in
Peru.

Some time earlier, Susan had met another prominent attorney called John O'Neill while up at Jim's
parents' cabin by the lake at Maxinkuckee. The moment Jim flew off for his fishing vacation, Susan drove
up to the lake and stayed at O'Neill's family home. It
was the beginning of a friendship that was to outlast
any other in her entire life.

One day, Susan felt it was time to tell Jim about her
"problems" in Oklahoma. Whether it was out of a

genuine inbuilt sense of guilt, or a blatant determination to wipe the slate clean and get back custody of her son, Jacob, no one will ever know. But there can be little doubt that Susan realized Jim Grund would have the connections to help her completely wipe out her past crimes.

Susan broke down in tears and told Jim the whole sob story about how unfairly she was treated in Oklahoma City. Jimmy Grund listened sympathetically and immediately began visitation rights hearings on Susan's son, Jacob. Susan had been most insistent that she wanted her son back, so they could all be one big, happy family. Jobless ex-husband Gary Campbell was soon struggling to pay out the vast sums of cash needed to fight Susan's legal efforts to win back custody of her son.

Then Susan put in a phone call to her ex-husband Campbell and *suggested* that he might like to move back to Indiana and get a job there. Gary was bemused by Susan's call. What was the point in him moving back? But Susan repeated her offer obviously convinced that she could persuade him to move to the Peru area.

Gary then came clean with his ex-wife and admitted he was living with a girl whom he had gotten pregnant. Susan listened intently on the other end of the phone line. This was brilliant news as far as she was concerned, because it meant that Gary was desperate. Instead of screaming at Gary, as he presumed she would, Susan decided to play the role of savior to her ex-husband.

"I could help you, Gary," she told him.

A few days later, Jimmy Grund wired over $800 to Campbell to pay for the girl to have an abortion. It was then that Susan realized she had regained complete control over the situation. She was negotiating from a position of strength and that made her feel very good indeed.

Shortly after the abortion, Jim Grund paid for Campbell to move to Indiana and an apartment to be found for him in nearby Logansport. It was not too close so that they had to keep meeting Campbell, but it was not so far that he would forget his obligations to Jimmy and Susan.

Gary was pleasantly surprised by both Susan and Jim's attitude towards him. However, he did not appreciate or understand their true motives. Grund even mentioned to Gary that he was thinking of offering him a job as manager of the airfield in Peru which he was planning to buy.

It is hardly surprising that the moment Campbell arrived back in Indiana, he relaxed his custody of Jacob and the child began spending more and more time with his mother. Campbell found it hard to object, because Susan was obviously more able to provide a stable home for the young boy.

Soon Susan enrolled Jacob in the local school in Peru. Meanwhile, Jim Grund even managed to find Campbell a minimum wage job driving a truck after his airport deal fell through. Susan was delighted. This whole maneuver was proving exactly what she had always believed—money means power. Without it, you might as well never have been born.

The next bit of good news came when Campbell fell in love with a local girl. Naturally, Susan suggested the happy couple should get married. It was taken for granted that Jim Grund would pay for the wedding expenses and reception. And guess who was the pro-tem judge on duty that day—attorney Jim Grund!

The service and reception were held in the Grund's

family house. Campbell's bride even wore the dress Susan had used when she married Jim Grund in Florida a year earlier.

Afterwards, Jim Grund gave Gary Campbell a $1500 cash gift that he called "a loan for tax purposes." The next day, Gary and his new bride rented a U-Haul trailer and moved back to Oklahoma City.

Shortly after this, the adoption order was removed and Jim Grund was able to legally adopt Susan's son Jacob. When the judge handling the case inquired as to the whereabouts of the real father, he was told Campbell had "disappeared." A legal notice was published in the local paper, but no one came forward.

Susan had manipulated the situation brilliantly. She had wooed and won over Gary Campbell because she wanted to buy back the love of her son Jacob. There was even talk that Susan had slept with Gary on a few occasions while she was "negotiating" the return of her son. Campbell always denied it happened, but a few of the Grunds' friends and family think otherwise.

Interestingly, Campbell did later admit he had sex with Susan during her earlier marriage to Tom Whited, but then she had been trying to get Campbell to allow her and her then husband to adopt Jacob as well, so her motivation, as usual, was loud and clear.

On that earlier occasion, Susan had insisted to Campbell that Whited came from a wealthy family and that Jacob would not be able to inherit anything unless he was adopted by Whited. But Gary refused to allow the adoption to go ahead. However, by the time Susan caught up with Gary Campbell following her marriage to Jim Grund it was a whole different ball game.

Jimmy Grund was also happy about the outcome over the custody of Jacob. He wanted a young family again to see if he could manage to bring up children without making the same mistakes he had made the first time around. His other priority was to make Susan happy. He had forgiven her for those appalling child battery accusations.

Not long afterwards, in a remarkable example of legal wheeler-dealing, Susan even got Jim to force the father of Tanelle—third husband Thomas Whited—to release all legal responsibilities for the little girl in exchange for a $25,000 payout. The money was to go into a trust fund for Tanelle to have when she grew up.

The most remarkable aspect of this is that Whited had witnessed first-hand the heartbreaking results of those beatings inflicted on his son Tommy, but still he played along with his ex-wife and her new, powerful lawyer husband.

At no stage during the negotiations did it enter Jim Grund's mind that Susan might be in any way using him. His main priority was the well-being of both of the children, whom he adored and treated as if they were his own.

Not long after this extraordinary deal with Whited was finalized, Jimmy Grund accepted paternity of Tanelle and then set up the trust fund for the child at the Peru Trust bank.

Susan's dream conversion toward social acceptability took another important turn when she persuaded Jim to buy a plot of land on Summit Drive, one of the most exclusive stretches of real estate in Peru.

At first, Jim had been reluctant to get involved in such a major construction project, but he realized that Susan needed something to do. She would get into a lot of trouble if he just left her at home, bored and frustrated. The house to be built on Summit Drive was the short-term answer, at least.

Susan for her part, was planning out her new career as a social butterfly with alarming precision. She knew it was important to keep Jim happy and satisfied and she enjoyed playing the attentive wife prepared to dress to perfection for even the most casual of dinner dates.

In bed, she made sure that Jimmy got all the satisfaction he could possibly require. Susan liked nothing more than to splash out hundreds of dollars at Victoria's Secret on skin-tight silky teddies and basques complete with sheer stockings and garter belts.

In the left-hand drawer of her closet chest of drawers she kept a sensual collection of black stockings, sheer lycra ones with a lace-effect top, denier stockings with a lace top that provided the perfect smooth, sheer, matte appearance. Susan also had black French lace suspender belts with matching high-cut panties, as well as other colored French lace suspender belts, also with matching high-cut panties.

All these items had been purchased by Susan throughout her many marriages and whenever she felt the urge for that kind of sexual healing response, she would make sure she wore them. All that silk underwear became a tool for Susan whenever the fancy took her. She had learned over the years that she could get pretty much whatever she wanted if she was prepared to seduce it out of her partner.

Essentially, she bought all this lingerie with the finest of intentions. It all began when one of her first lovers suggested she wear stockings and suspenders in bed one time. Susan soon learnt that there was only one kind of man: the man who loves stockings. She realized it was a universal impulse on their part.

Sooner or later all her lovers and husbands would
expect her to "wear the stockings." Usually it was
around the same time they wanted to know how many
previous lovers she had had. It was inevitable.

After that first time, Susan felt that stockings were
a very useful prop when it came to getting what she
wanted. Soon she did not have to be asked by her
partner because she would start the day by slipping
into a skin-tight silky basque and stockings. It started
to make her feel good and she grew especially fond of
providing men with a glimpse of basque or stocking
top, aware that it would make them feel immensely
excited.

Sometimes, Susan would cook Jim Grund a candle-
lit dinner and allow her tight pencil skirt to ride just
high enough up her thigh to reveal her stocking top,
just to make sure she got exactly what she wanted
from her husband.

And to ensure that Susan was never far from
Jimmy, even when he went off on his regular all-male
fishing jaunts to places like Mexico and Canada, Susan had some startlingly sexy photos taken of herself
in some of that Victoria's Secret underwear. She insisted he take one of the sexiest shots with him on
every overnight trip he ever made.

Back at the construction site up on Summit Drive,
Susan briefed the builders of the house constantly.
She droned on about painting the inside of the property "New York white," but the puzzled construction
workers just could not fathom what the difference was
between that and normal white.

Compared to the other houses in the area, this one
was its plain sister, even though it was probably the
biggest property. While others were artfully land-

scaped, the Grund residence had only a few scraggly shrubs surrounding it. A number of immature trees flopped awkwardly across the front yard. The dwelling, while obviously expensively constructed, had no character or personality, more closely resembling an apartment block than the home of one of the most prominent members of Peru's upper class.

Looking at the house itself—which was built between January and May 1986—it appeared to be a two-storey structure. But there was a level below, which included a laundry room and a playroom for children. The house ended up a carefully designed mansion that was most notable for its complete lack of atmosphere. Susan's obsession with neatness meant that any friendly or familiar possessions were banned from shelves, which then lay permanently bare. But that was the way Susan wanted it. She hated clutter because clutter reminded her of her childhood. That house represented a major achievement for Susan. It was a long way from her neighborhood and every time she summoned forth a mental image of her own family home and compared it to the vast dwelling where she now lived, it brought a wry smile to her face. Up here, she said to herself, things *are* different. The paint looks fresher, the lawns thicker, the shade cooler, the foliage more lush. I have truly arrived, thought Susan, reflecting on how she had brilliantly put all that poverty and misery behind her. The past now seemed all a blur, inconsequential compared to the mental and physical ordeal she was going to continue in order to kick all those old embarrassing habits and friends.

The house, with its superb views and hand designed amenities lacked something else that Susan considered the ultimate social symbol—a decent-sized swimming pool. Jim Grund had insisted they could only afford a hot tub and to make matters even more shaming for Susan, he had bought one cheap from a friend. But then that was typical of Jim.

While Susan liked to hand pick the perfect car, Jim drove the same Delta 88, with its slit in the old, bubbling vinyl roof, for years. As far as he was concerned, it worked fine, so what was the point in changing it?

Soon after the main construction of the house was completed, Susan and Jim had a blazing row that resulted in her moving all her belongings out of the marital bedroom.

It all started when Jim refused to build a separate walk-in closet for Susan to put her clothes in. They had enjoyed a similar arrangement at their previous home and it had proved very irritating to Susan, who took great pride in looking after her clothes very carefully and objected to sharing hanging facilities with a sloppy man like Jim, whose only interest in clothes were that they be functional.

When builders came to carry out some finishing touches on the new house, Jim insisted on him and Susan just having one, extra-long closet between them. On the day they were scheduled to move in all their clothes, Susan had gone shopping and returned to fill her half of the closet with her clothes. She moved Jim's clothes down a little and managed to take up a lot more space than him.

When Jim arrived home that evening, he got really angry at Susan's invasion of his space and shouted at her, "I told you, you can't have any more of my closet."

She snapped back, "Well, I told you before that I didn't want to build this closet and I wanted it bigger and so, if I can't have my closet, then I'll just take all my clothes out and put 'em in the guest bedroom."

And that's exactly what she did. Susan picked all her clothes up and marched them into the guest bedroom. Susan and Jim slept in separate bedrooms that night. Down the hallway, little Jacob heard them arguing and it reminded him of those awful, terror-filled days back on Rushing Road, Oklahoma City, when his stepbrother got beaten so severely.

After Jacob heard his mother shouting in a fit of temper, he started sobbing quietly into his pillow because he had been through that sort of heartache too many times already.

The house on Summit Drive cost a total of $175,000 by the time it was finished to Susan's very unimaginative specifications. Almost every room other than the kitchen was covered in thick, plush white carpet that showed every stain or crumb. Susan would always be barking at the children to take off their shoes the moment they walked in the house and she often used to shout similar orders at grown-ups, too.

Most of the walls were uncovered apart from the occasional picture of Susan herself. The centerpiece of the entire house was Susan and Jim's double bedroom, complete with a vast, specially commissioned portrait of herself in the nude. That picture cost Jim Grund more than $3,000. The bedroom also became the prime setting for the countless Polaroid snaps Susan continued to take of herself in the nude or scantily clad. At first, they were given to Jim as a reminder of how sexy she was, but gradually they became more like manipulative tools provided specifically by Susan to taunt her husband when he was feeling particularly insecure about her friendships with other men.

Susan even insisted her new husband have a photo of her, scantily clad, in his office. It was a running joke amongst his colleagues, but he kept it there all the same because he knew that Susan was liable to pop round unannounced at the office and then completely freak out if the photo was not prominently displayed.

# Six

Jim Grund's gawky teenage son David moved into the house on Summit soon after it was completed. But he did not get on with either his father or stepmother at the time and by the summer of 1986 they kicked him out and told him to go back to Jim's ex-wife, Jane.

There had been constant rows with David about money and Susan seemed to be forever finding herself stuck in the middle whenever Jim and his son argued. She was infuriated by David's complete lack of interest in keeping his room tidy. Sometimes she felt like hitting him, just as she had done with poor little Tommy three years earlier. But even she realized that David was a little too large to inflict punishment on without risking a beating in return.

Once Susan acknowledged this, she tried to turn around her role in the family, and David started to look on Susan as the family pacifier. For every row he had with his father, she seemed to be the problem solver. Frequently, she cooled down difficult situations when Jim Grund and his son would almost come to blows.

But then, in David's eyes, it was easy for his stepmother to play that role since she seemed to have a never-ending source of money from Jim Grund. While his father appeared tightfisted about splashing out cash on his son, Jim Grund seemed like putty in Susan's hands whenever she wanted a new dress, or whatever. That underlying tension sparked many rows between David and his father and the boy found it even more irritating that Susan played up her role as the considerate stepmom when she was actually the cause of most of the problems. It was a constantly changing set of emotions. One minute, David was angry at his stepmother, the next he was grateful that at least she had the courage to step between him and his father. Rest assured, Susan knew exactly what she was doing throughout this period.

It had been inevitable that Susan and Jim would decide David had to go back to his mother's home. The tension in the house had become far too much of a strain for any of them to cope with. There was a genuine fear that some physical harm might come to one of them if they continued trying to coexist in that vast house on Summit Drive, which David saw as the ultimate evidence of his father's over generosity toward Susan. But the true extent of David's love-hate relationship with his glamorous stepmother had not yet fully developed.

Throughout those early years of his marriage to Susan, Jimmy Grund steadfastly held on to the independence he had enjoyed throughout most of his adult life. At least twice a year, he would fly his six-passenger Lance Piper plane up to places like Charrington

Lake, Ontario, with some of his good male friends such as Peru Police Sgt. Gary Nichols, his fellow lawyer Don Fern, and business partner Don Bakehorn.

Susan accepted that these journeys were entirely innocent, male-bonding trips—and in any case they invariably gave her an opportunity to go out and party while Jim was away. She had already made a close friend in attorney John O'Neill during an earlier occasion when Jim was away. But now she had a vast mansion on the best side of town to call her own, and she fully intended to entertain in style.

During those first few years of their marriage, Jim adored seeing Susan act and dress sexy whenever they went out. It was almost as if he was saying to the rest of the community, "Look at her but don't touch, 'cause she's mine and no one else can have her." He rewarded her with a monthly allowance of almost $1,000 to spend on whatever she liked. It was more than Susan had ever earned at any of the menial jobs she had worked since leaving school.

But the tide turned in the late 1980s when Susan started going out to functions in Indianapolis on her own because Jim wasn't interested—or sometimes wasn't even invited. On a number of occasions, Susan would make it plain that her husband was not smart enough to be seen on her arm. It was all a long way from those days when Susan believed that Jim was going to provide her with the perfect ladder to ascend to social acceptability.

There was also another side of Susan's character that was beginning to emerge. Some nights she liked to dress up in body-hugging black leather skirts and meet certain girlfriends and men friends at local clip joints like The Ice House. Susan really enjoyed the sensation of knowing that as she maneuvered across the crowded clubs, men's eyes would be locked on her body, watching every curve.

Susan's real background did occasionally come through, thanks to her rather inept taste in clothes. Sometimes, on those nights out she would mix the wrong colors or wear cheap, dangly jewelry with chic dresses. Often she would be wearing a see-through top showing off her ample breasts, which many of her associates believed had been injected with silicone to improve their shape. Susan always wore plenty of cosmetics, although they were applied with sublety where possible.

Susan's trips into sleaziness seemed to be a release from her daytime image as the finely coiffured lady of good taste married to the respectable lawyer with the huge house up on the hill. Certain low-life acquaintances would join her in these clip joints but she didn't get drunk or take drugs. That definitely wasn't Susan's way of dealing with things. She had never actually been drunk in her life. She didn't like to lose control, ever. But these trips to the other side were like a catharsis, enabling her to let herself go and be herself just for a few hours. And when Susan Grund decided to be her old, slutty self, any man in the room had to beware because she needed a conquest like others need a new hairstyle.

Back on the respectable daytime Peru social scene, Susan was continuing to make inroads at an impressive pace. One of her friends even introduced her to a senator one day at a social function at Peru's oldest and most respected bed-and-breakfast establishment, the Rosewood Mansion.

Susan felt a tingle of excitement run up her body the moment she met this rich and famous man. He represented an even more potent ride away from her upbringing on the other side of the tracks than Jimmy Grund. But she decided not to be too forward this time. She knew that if she was going to stand any chance with a man of this standing then she would have to take her time. Instant sexual gratification was not going to get her a free ride into Washington.

Susan also started running a number of local beauty pageants because she knew it was a good way to climb to even greater social heights. Meanwhile, Jimmy Grund remained completely unimpressed, much to her frustration and annoyance. He was happy that Susan had something to occupy her day, but he did not give a fig about the social scene in Peru because he had been part of it from the day he was born. He had seen right through it years earlier and he had absolutely nothing to prove.

Then Susan persuaded Jim to financially back a boutique she wanted to open in the center of town. Initially, Jim ploughed at least $25,000 into the business.

Susan was ecstatically happy because the store— called Clothes by Susan—further elevated her social standing in the community. Now, she was not only the wife of a very successful lawyer, but she was also a businesswoman in her own right.

But others were watching her entrance into the fashion world with more than just a hint of skepticism. Her stepson David was irritated because his father was always pleading poverty when it came to allowances. Yet it was clear to David that his father had ploughed most of his available cash into that boutique. It caused a further rift that took father and son several months to heal. Ironically, once that rupture was smoothed over, Susan's relationship with David started to improve beyond anyone's expectations.

April 4, 1989, was the fifteenth official day of spring in Peru and Susan Grund was feeling full of the joys of life. Her relentless pursuit of the title as most social lady in town was fast becoming a reality.

On the breakfast table that morning she was positively glowing as she read a report in the Peru edition of the *Kokomo Tribune* headlined, WOMEN TO VIE FOR TITLE.

The piece kicked off, "Two north central Indiana women are amongst entrants in the 1989 Mrs. Indiana America Pageant to be presented in the Grand Ballroom of the Hilton at the airport in Indianapolis on April 15 and 16.

"Elizabeth Griffey of Delphi and Susan Grund of Peru will compete at the state pageant where Indiana's representative to the Mrs. America Pageant will be selected."

Susan was thrilled. Her only complaint was that her name was not ahead of Mrs. Griffey in the report.

The article informed its readers, "Susan is married to James H. Grund, a lawyer in Peru. They have two children, Jacob and Tanelle."

The report also stated that amongst Susan's sponsors for the pageant was Gary Nichols, the police officer who arranged the blind date on which she first met Jim Grund.

Less than three months later, Susan managed not just one, but two photos in the same issue of the local newspaper as she taught youngsters how to hold themselves for the 4-H Miss Miami Queen contest, as well as the 4-H Little Miss Queen competition. Everyone at the paper noticed how incredibly photogenic Susan was.

But there was another side to Susan during this period. She was becoming increasingly restless about her life in Peru. Their beautiful house was complete. She had a generous allowance from Jimmy that had just gone up to $2,000 a month. He was out at work from dawn till dusk every day and often later. Life needed a new challenge for Susan. She had been on her best behavior for a couple of years now. Perhaps it was time to find a new bed partner.

Susan was spurred on by the fact that she felt unsatisfied by her sex life with Jim. She complained to one girlfriend about his inability to get an erection and she made it plainly obvious that if an opportunity for an extramarital affair came along she would grab at the chance.

Initially, she began a steamy illicit liaison with an accountant in a nearby town. This was naturally kept secret from almost all Susan's family and friends at the time. She did not want to risk ending her marriage to Jim, but she just felt the urge for a bit of excitement.

She had first met her new lover when he did some accounting work for her. At first, Susan and her new friend had a few innocent lunches together with other businessmen in nearby Logansport.

Then Susan began making sexual advances toward the man and he submitted. There followed a passionate yet impersonal affair that resulted in them having sex on at least a dozen occasions. Sometimes they met in motels, but on at least three occasions they made love at Susan's sister's house in Kokomo, including one incident when her nephew Paul arrived home early from school to find his aunt naked in bed with her lover.

The affair with the accountant was completely non-threatening to Susan's marriage. She looked on it as a way to gain sexual satisfaction without hurting anyone. In fact, it was so casual that the couple would often go for as long as two months without actually meeting.

Eventually, the affair fizzled out because Susan's lover felt guilty about his business relationship with Jimmy Grund. But he never forgot how Susan would openly talk about her sexual prowess. It was almost as if Susan enjoyed telling her men friends about her sexual kicks just to keep them on their toes and to make sure they knew that she did not need them that badly because there were plenty more where they came from.

But one prospective lover who did get away was an extremely handsome choreographer for a local cheerleading team. He had first met Susan when she had driven with a friend and her husband to Indianapolis for a ballgame and they all ended up going out for dinner and dancing. That evening, Susan was wearing a very sexy dress with seamed stockings and spiky three-inch patent leather black pumps. Throughout the night she kept telling the choreographer how open her marriage was and how she was free to have as many bedmates as she wanted. She also let slip that her husband did not even know where she was because he was away on a fishing trip at the time.

Later on, Susan and the man went to a friend's apartment in Indianapolis. The friend was out of town for the night. The moment the choreographer and Susan lay on the bed to watch television, she grabbed him and started fondling him. The man then stopped Susan and told her that he was gay and had a male lover and wasn't interested in women.

Susan was astounded, but tried again to excite the

man. In the end, she gave up and drove home to Peru early the next morning.

A few months later, Susan introduced the man to Jimmy Grund at a fund-raising event in the Peru area and they got on well. Grund even seriously considered putting up cash to fund a dance studio the man wanted to open in Peru.

Word of Susan's attempt to seduce this man swept around Shanty Malone's bar like wildfire. It became a running joke amongst regulars—including many of Jim's closest friends—that over-sexed Susan had tried to seduce a homosexual.

And throughout all this extramarital activity, Susan was continuing to make quite a name for herself on the Peru social scene. She remained a regular in the society columns of the local newspaper and even wrote a letter to the editor complimenting him on a humorous article published the previous week. She was positively bursting with enthusiasm for the community of which she was now such a major part.

In the letter—dated December 13, 1989—she wrote, "We are a small but proud community. It is nice to be friendly. Welcome to Peru."

It was fairly sickly sweet in its wordage, but that was the image Susan was desperate to project in Peru. She knew there were a few people around who loved to drag up her past life from when she lived on the wrong side of the tracks. But she was out to prove that she was as classy as any lady in Peru.

Local society columnist Nancy Newman was most impressed by Susan Grund who went to a great deal of trouble during her involvement with the Miami County Orange Queen pageant. Susan would groom the girls, organize the publicity, chaperone the entrants, and teach them how to walk and how to handle dates with boys.

Nancy Newman was convinced Susan was very nice to someone if she wanted something. But she would often pass people on the street whom she had met previously and not utter so much as a hello.

Susan was also known to some reporters on the local papers as a feisty lady who did not hesitate to make their lives a misery if they refused to plant something in the press for her.

And she seemed to have a near-obsession with the activities of the family who owned the *Peru Daily Tribune.* Nancy Newman was told off by Susan one day because she did not know where her house on Summit Drive was located. "But that's where the family that owns your newspaper lives," exclaimed Susan to her journalist friend.

Nancy Newman was a rare example of someone in Peru who knew all about Susan's impoverished background. She had regularly met with Susan's retarded brother Eddie and her father, William, at a sheltered workshop for backward children in Peru many years before.

Despite Susan's attempts to pretend her father barely existed, William was known to quite a number of people in Peru as a very simple but gentle man, nothing like the brutal image portrayed by his daughter.

Not long after this, Susan persuaded Jimmy Grund to put even more cash into her clothing boutique in Peru. She even bragged to one friend that she had partly financed Clothes by Susan by forging Jim's name to get another $10,000 loan for extra stock.

Around this time, Susan went on a clothes buying

trip to Chicago with her close friend Terri Mettica, who ran a similar store in nearby Logansport. Terri could not help noticing how Susan flirted with all the clothing wholesalers they met during their trip. She made a point of wearing low-cut dresses and Terri reckoned that most of the men they dealt with hardly even noticed her because Susan was coming on so strong.

Only a few months later, Susan's store burned to the ground in a mysterious fire. Within hours of the blaze, Susan admitted to close friend Terri that she did not have proper insurance coverage and she was financially ruined.

A week later, Terri got another call from Susan. This time she said she did have insurance and she wanted Terri to supply her with invoices from her store so Susan could collect from the insurance company.

The Peru Fire Department proclaimed the blaze unsolved, but admitted there were definite question marks over how it was caused. However no one was ever prosecuted for starting the fire.

Susan's great friendship with Terri Mettica grew because she truly thought she had found a real soulmate in Terri, who openly admitted her motto in life was, *The obvious is least obvious.* Terri reckoned that if you wanted to flirt in front of your husband then you should go right ahead and do it because then he is more than likely to get the impression nothing is going on. Susan rapidly applied this motto to herself.

Susan became more and more blatant about her illicit sexual liaisons. In a perverse way, she firmly believed that if you wanted something hidden, then if you did the most obvious thing, no one would ever suspect you. It was a strange attitude to take because she was clearly implying it was better to rub your partner's nose in it than bother to carry out affairs in secret.

Susan stunned one friend who was considering an affair herself by describing in detail how, if you want to cheat on your husband then you should invite your boyfriend over or call him when your husband is listening and then if you get caught your husband would never suspect anything. Susan's track record in these matters was rather questionable.

Susan also got into the habit with her closest girlfriends of joking about killing Jim and easily getting away with it because "it would be so obvious it was me." These proclamations would come completely out of the blue.

Susan really shocked one friend by bragging about the sordid details of a particularly passionate affair and saying she could easily break up her lover's marriage, but he didn't make enough money for her to bother doing it. Once again, money was the dominant theme in any relationship for Susan.

But, in her numerous sexual adventures throughout Indiana, there continued to be the occasional reassuring rejection that disproved most women's beliefs that men cannot resist a promiscuous female. In other words, there were still some men who ran a mile when Susan made a pass at them.

One time, she got so obsessed with a doctor in Indianapolis that she went out for lunch with him wearing a sheer red silk teddy under her dress in the hope that they would end up in bed together that afternoon. The doctor turned down her advances over lunch, but Susan insisted to friends for months afterwards that they were having an affair and that she was going to fly somewhere exotic with him on a vacation. It was all a fantasy.

She created an entire sexual liaison that she retold in vivid, explicit detail to her closest friends. It was clear that Susan got almost as much sexual excitement out of the fantasy side of her life as the reality.

In the end, the doctor in Indianapolis had to refer Susan to a much more elderly doctor for her health problems because he felt so uncomfortable in her presence.

Susan openly talked about divorcing Jim because she was not happy with him, but underneath it all she realized that she wouldn't get much of a financial settlement from Jim because they did not have their own children. In any case, he did not have much spare cash floating around. It was tied up in a plane, a half share in Shanty Malone's bar, and a number of other smaller investments.

Susan also continued repeating to her friends a degrading story about Jim failing to get an erection when they were in bed together. It was as if she was trying to defend her reasons for finding sexual gratification elsewhere. But not once did she stop and think about what might have caused his sexual problems. Perhaps it was because he did not love her any more.

Gossip about Susan's extramarital escapades continued to spread through Peru at a furious pace. One of their neighbors up at that secluded house on Summit Drive got the shock of her life when she spotted Susan French-kissing a man at the local fairgrounds.

That same neighbor's daughter baby-sat for the Grunds and she reported to her mother that Susan was always going out dressed to the nines when her husband was away on fishing trips. Often, Susan would not return until the early hours of the morning.

But Susan firmly believed in one law for her and another for her husband if he ever dared be unfaithful to her.

Susan told her friend Zoyla Henderson that if she ever caught Jim with anyone she would kill him, although many years later she insisted the remark was said entirely in jest.


Jim and Susan were certainly on the "A" list when it came to parties in Peru. And some of those hog roasts and cook-outs tended to be pretty wild affairs.

Often there was skinny-dipping, pot smoking, and sometimes even some cocaine available at the adult get-togethers, although neither Jim nor Susan was ever seen taking any drugs at these events.

Susan was known to many local housewives as someone definitely not to leave alone with your husband. Women had a bad feeling about Susan. They felt she was always on the prowl, looking out for a man to seduce and then use and abuse and destroy. Many of the women suspected that Susan was having numerous affairs at any one time. At some of the more outrageous parties, Susan would proudly strip off her clothes and show off her great body before diving into a swimming pool as naturally as a duck into water.

There were also times when Jim Grund went off on his own, too. Sometimes he would hang out at the tiny bar at the Peru Airport on the edge of town. He kept his own plane there for many years and enjoyed sampling a few beers after arriving back from some trip or other.

There were usually a few women at the Peru Airport bar including Shirley Day, owner of the popular D and D lounge in Peru. One night some of the regulars were drinking way past licensing hours when a plane flew in with Jimmy Grund at the controls. After unloading a vast number of boxes, Grund rolled in and ordered himself a beer. He never did discuss what was in those boxes.

In 1989, Susan was delighted when Jim agreed to go into partnership with his brother-in-law Fred Allen in a car dealership business. She was particularly pleased because part of the deal was that she would be provided with a new model every month.

That year, Jim and Susan went on a vacation to Florida with his sister Jane and husband Fred to celebrate the new business venture. One day, everyone was out by the pool of the hotel when Jane noticed scars on Susan's breasts that seemed to suggest she had implants. It was also fairly obvious because Susan's breasts seemed to stand at attention the entire time.

In the end, Fred could not resist making a comment.

"How much did those things cost, Susan?"

Susan looked furious and snapped back, "How would I know, I've never had mine done."

On that vacation, Jimmy's sister Jane came to the conclusion that one of Susan's biggest problems was her complete lack of a sense of humor. She just did not get it when other people told gags—especially if they were about her. She seemed to have no basic understanding of irony. She was only capable of seeing things in one narrow dimension. It was black or it was white, but there were definitely no gray areas in Susan's mind, unlike her life.

That humor defect and the continuing stories about Susan's sexual escapades were really beginning to concern Jim's mother, Connie. So, a few weeks later, she even went as far as confronting her son about Susan and especially about her apparent propensity for men.

Jimmy Grund hesitated for a moment and then made a strange comment: "All I can say is that I have never found anything she has told me to be untrue."

Connie Grund was puzzled by her son's reply because she had not even been suggesting Susan was a liar, but somehow he had felt obligated to give that response.

Meanwhile, Susan's numerous relatives from the wrong side of the tracks continued to enjoy all that Jimmy Grund could offer in the way of luxurious amenities.

On Thursday, January 18, 1990, Susan's sister Rita married Robert Saylors at the Grund home on Summit Drive. Naturally, Jimmy Grund—who just happened to be judge pro-tem on that day—officiated at the ceremony.

Rita was given away in marriage by her son Paul, the same youth who had found Susan in bed with a man a few months earlier. The reception that followed at the house for more than fifty people probably put Jimmy Grund back to the tune of at least $2,000.

On April 23, 1990, an incident occurred that had a disastrous long-term effect on Susan Grund when she called the police to report a burglary that afternoon at the house up on Summit Drive.

At approximately 3:58 P.M. State Trooper Michael Brown arrived at the Miami County Sheriff's office to be greeted by then Sheriff Don Howard and Jimmy Grund. They had just received a call from Susan

Grund stating that the residence had been burglarized and she was scared that someone might still be inside the house.

An anxious Jimmy Grund suggested to Brown that he get over there as quickly as possible.

At 4:02 P.M. Brown and Dep. Jan Kendall screeched to a halt outside the house on Summit to find Susan Grund outside. They immediately entered the house and checked each room for a perpetrator. Kendall ventured carefully round the house, mindful of the dispatcher's warning that a burglar might be still inside. Glancing in the rooms on the ground level and finding them empty, Kendall headed for the main bedroom where he found what appeared to be evidence of a break-in.

At 4:41 P.M. State Trooper Investigator Robert Brinson arrived at the house to handle the investigation.

Bob Brinson was well aware that the house belonged to one time county prosecutor Jimmy Grund and his young, attractive second wife and he also realized that his superiors would be expecting an especially thorough job on this particular investigation because of the high society folk involved.

In fact, Brinson had called at the house a few months earlier when Susan's dinky little Fiat sportscar was daubed in red paint by a vandal. There was talk of it being done by local kids, but in the end, the investigation ran out of steam although Bob Brinson could still remember it vividly.

Brinson immediately met with Jim Grund and Susan at the house that day and started a careful examination of the property. He discovered one of the windows in the master bedroom was open and it appeared to have been cut to allow entry. Jimmy Grund assured Brinson that the window was definitely locked earlier that day.

But Brinson noted that due to the construction of the casement-type window it would be nearly impossible for a burglar to gain entry through it if it had not been left open in the first place. Brinson also noticed there were no pry marks on the window frame and the screen wire on the bottom of the frame had not been disturbed. He found it very unlikely that a burglar could enter the house via the screen window and not disturb or cut the wire.

On examining the bedroom, the first thing that struck Brinson was the word PRICK emblazoned above the couple's double bed in black spray paint. Brinson's scene of the crime specialist colleague Sgt. Dean Marks carefully took a sample of the wallpaper for evidence. There was no sign of the paint spray can although the Grunds said they had used something similar in recent days to paint a child's toy.

Jimmy Grund then went on to tell Brinson that he was missing an 8x10 size photograph of Susan modeling a swimsuit at a fashion show. The photo had been in a gold frame. Brinson was a bit mystified by the fact that nothing else appeared to have been disturbed in the bedroom.

Next, he headed for the Grund's vast walk-in closet next to the master bathroom. Looking at obvious signs of disturbance, Susan Grund informed Brinson that about twenty sets of lingerie, mainly from Victoria's Secret, were missing. Then she went on to mention gold necklaces, matching bracelets, rings, and earrings. Susan claimed the jewelry had been taken from a wooden jewelry box with mirror side doors. Jim Grund then chipped in that the burglar had also ransacked four drawers in his clothes chest. However, although the bottom two drawers were partially open, nothing had actually been disturbed. There were other things that had been moved around in the closet, but no other items appeared stolen.

Then Jim Grund announced that he was missing one hundred twenty-dollar bills from one drawer.

Brinson later noted in his scene-of-the-crime report that he was surprised none of Jim Grund's jewelry had been taken. There had also been several silver dollars in the opened jewelry box, but they had not been taken either.

No other part of the house appeared to have been touched and nothing else was missing. Brinson then noted that the living room patio door was open and so it appeared the burglar had left through that exit.

Just as Bob Brinson was about to wrap up his inquiries for the day, Susan's nephew Paul arrived at the house after finishing his shift at a local Wendy's restaurant. Paul was living with the Grunds and attending high school in Kokomo for his senior year.

Paul told Brinson he had been home briefly at noon after finishing school before setting off for his job, returning at 2:00 P.M. to get something to eat before heading back to work at 2:30 P.M. Brinson later contacted the manager of Wendy's who confirmed Paul's movements.

Then Paul dropped a minor bombshell by admitting that he had spent part of that afternoon in the company of a man who was awaiting trial in Miami County for robbery and who had a lengthy past criminal record. Brinson was astounded to hear that the nephew of two such prominent Peru residents should be mixing with such a disreputable character. He decided he had to investigate Paul's involvement.

Brinson then headed for Shanty Malone's bar,

which Jim Grund part-owned, and where Paul told them this other suspected criminal was enjoying a drink. On arrival, Brinson and his investigators talked to the man and then escorted him to his girlfriend's trailer and interviewed her about his movements. Both of them insisted they knew nothing about the burglary at Summit Drive and Brinson tended to believe them. It was far too obvious a scenario, although he did get an assurance from the couple that they would be available for a polygraph test if required.

On April 27, 1990, Brinson persuaded Susan's nephew Paul Sanders to agree to a polygraph to clear his name. The test took place at the Indiana State Police Post in Peru, and was carried out by Sgt. Mark James. Paul passed with flying colors.

But when Brinson tried to persuade Susan Grund to take a polygraph she was outraged and refused point-blank to even consider it.

On May 2, Paul's friend with a criminal record was also polygraph tested. The results were "inconclusive" but Brinson and his investigators concluded that the man was afraid of the police because of previous encounters and this could have caused his apparent failure. Polygraph examiner Sergeant James even assured Bob Brinson that in his opinion the suspect was being truthful. That was enough for Brinson. He concluded in his eventual report that "this unit has no additional leads to follow and therefore will suspend the investigation at this time."

Bob Brinson had his own suspicions about who was probably responsible for the break-in, but he wasn't about to risk his career by making his feelings known in public.

He duly noted that a hefty insurance claim was made on the damaged and missing items, and Susan

Grund got her bedroom beautifully redecorated at no cost to herself. Brinson actually thought that maybe Susan had staged the break-in to make her husband feel sorry for her. There has to be an easier way to keep a marriage intact, thought Brinson.

# Seven

Susan's biggest problem was sex. Although gossip later focused heavily on her admittedly active bedtime activities, those who knew her painted a picture of a much more complex personality, a woman with widely divergent mood swings and contradictory behavior patterns.

When she wanted to, it seemed, or when it suited her purposes, she could be sweet, loving, and thoughtful. When, in 1990, her parents divorced after more than forty years of marriage, she was the first one to go rushing to her mother's side offering every type of support. The divorce was a complete bolt out of the blue, but the entire family soon accepted it as a fact of life.

Jim's law practice partner Don Fern represented Susan's mother Nellie in the divorce after a special deal was agreed upon so that it cost Nellie virtually nothing in legal fees. Fern had always felt a little hesitant about his partner's wife, but dealing with her during her mother's divorce simply confirmed his dislike

of her. He found that Susan was forever telling him
how to do his job.

Susan's mother Nellie wasn't particularly upset by
the breakup of her marriage. She just decided it was
time to end an unhappy relationship. They had nothing in common and now the children had all left home
what else was there for them?

Susan's father William was heartbroken, though.
He suddenly found himself cut off from his family.
With no one to turn to, he headed off west for Texas
and then Arizona, drifting from town to town, surviv-
ing on a disability allowance.

A few months later he committed suicide. No one
really knows why, but most of the family believe he
was distraught about the end of the marriage.
Whether or not he ever abused any of his children or
caused them any other real suffering would never be
accurately established.

But one thing is known for certain—Jimmy Grund
paid for his father-in-law's funeral expenses.

Meanwhile, Jimmy Grund was working hard as ever
as a busy attorney. Often he would come home at
night and pour out all the details of his most interesting cases to a riveted Susan. She was fascinated. She
had now been on both sides of the law and she felt she
had a good handle on what an ass it could be at times.

Sometimes, Susan would surprise Jim by making
some very salient points about the legal ramifications
of a particular case. She was especially fond of hearing all the gory details of gruesome murder trials.

"But you don't wanna hear all that grisly stuff, do
you?" Jim would ask.

"I do, honey," replied Susan in her finest, softest
Southern drawl. "I really do."

One time, Jim told his wife all about a truly horrendous case of a man who kept a body in a sleeping bag and had sex with the corpse everywhere. The man had been living at home with his parents and was considered something of a daddy's boy. Susan was captivated by the case and pleaded with her husband to tell her all the details.

Susan was actually storing all these cases neatly in a fragment of her brain where she could reimagine them at any later stage she wanted. She needed to know all the tricks of the trade. She was desperate to understand the best way to commit the perfect murder.

Around this time, Susan had yet more dealings with Bob Brinson of the Indiana State Police when she asked for an officer to come to the house on Summit whilst Jimmy was away on one of his regular fishing jaunts to Canada. Brinson appeared at the house on Summit Drive to find Susan wearing a very low-cut dress and complaining about a flat tire. Brinson did not stay long enough to find out exactly what her intentions were.

In October 1990, further evidence of the Grund's crumbling marriage came from a most unlikely source—a fifth birthday party for Jim's sister Jane's son, Brad.

In an extraordinarily candid moment, Fred Allen—Jane's husband—pointed his home videocamera directly at the couple as they were arguing about Susan's favorite subject, cars.

The camera caught Jim and Susan deep in conversation. She asked him dryly, "What happened to my car?"

"Buy junk, you live with it, I guess," came Jim's stoic reply.

But then Susan barked back, *"Oh, I'm used to living with junk."*

A few miles and half a world away, while the impeccably clad, politically conscious members of Peru's legal community sipped white wine or vodka and nibbled daintily from each other's smorgasboards, Susan's sister Rita—still firmly entrenched on the wrong side of the tracks—was listening with astonishment to her sister on the phone.

"I'm having an affair with David."

Susan's words to her sister Rita were so laid back that it was as if she was talking about the weather. Rita was not that surprised, though. She had always been well aware of her sister's obsession with men and had even provided Susan with a love nest at her apartment in Kokomo where she would frequently bring her men friends. But all the same, to hear that she had started a relationship with her husband's son seemed a little excessive.

Susan claimed the first time she made love to David was when the two younger children spent the night over at friends' houses. David and she had been out for dinner together while Jim Grund was away. When they returned to the empty, isolated house on Summit Drive the couple had gone to the bedroom to watch television because there wasn't a set in the living room area. Within minutes of entering the bedroom they were making love, insisted Susan.

Another friend who allegedly was aware of the affair was Shirley Day. She actually lodged for a while with Susan's family at their house on 3rd Street. And she found herself regularly getting into late-night conversations with the rest of the Sanders family over the topic of Susan's affair with her stepson David. There was a general impression that this time Susan had gone too far. The family wanted her to stop the relationship, but Susan had told them in no uncertain terms to mind their own business.

A few weeks later, Shirley claims she saw Susan out in the street with her stepson. They stopped by a store window and then snatched a brief kiss on the lips. She had no doubt that Susan had embarked on a very passionate relationship.

By the following summer of 1991, this highly illicit affair had become, claimed Susan, a very regular sexual liaison. David was getting close to the end of his college year and he would spend Fridays with his stepmother during which they would enjoy passionate sex sessions, if what Susan has said is to be believed.

More often than not the love-making would, Susan later alleged, take place at the house on Summit Drive. But sometimes she would go to his home in Peru when his then girlfriend Monica Weaver was not around. When David dropped Monica for attractive Suzanne Plunkett it made no difference to his affair with Susan. They just carried on.

In late June of 1991, Susan made sure the grand house on Summit was empty all day, so that she could give her illicit lover a very special birthday present; they stayed in bed virtually the entire day.

Susan made sure her sister Darlene and her mother were also well aware of the alleged relationship with David, because she had gone to great lengths to ensure they knew all the details. Susan's mother Nellie was bemused by the entire episode, but she had long since stopped being surprised by anything her wayward daughter ever did.

Meanwhile, other Peru residents seemed aware that something was going on between Susan and David. It was becoming a topic of conversation amongst a number of her housewifely acquaintances.

On the Peru social scene, Susan was delighted when she found her photograph spread across page two of the *Peru Daily Tribune* on August 12, 1991. This time she was pictured presenting a second place divisional award for the Frances Slocum Bank's Circus City Festival parade float. Susan positively glowed in the picture and managed to dominate the shot much more than pretty young 1991 Miss Miami County, Cami Lowrance.

Another aspect of her minicelebrity in town was that it opened doors to high places for Susan. She was becoming increasingly supportive to that local senator she had befriended, although she did tend to drop a few clangers in conversation with him. One classic example was when the senator asked her what she did for a living.

"My full-time job is to set Jim up so well that if he ever leaves me, he'll leave with nothing."

The senator made a note not to ever cross this particular lady.

In April 1991, Susan filed a complaint with the Indiana Bell Telephone security department about a number of threatening calls that had been made to the house on Summit Drive. A trap was installed by the phone company, but Susan never actually filed a log of any more obscene calls as she had been instructed to do and the entire incident just fizzled out.

But then two months later she started making fresh allegations about threatening calls and Indiana Bell mailed a complaint form to her house, but it was never returned and the police were not contacted. It appeared to just fade out.

Jim was so concerned he called his friend police Sgt. Gary Nichols—an expert wiretapper—and arranged for his phone to be monitored with a tape recorder to try and find out who was making all the calls. Jim Grund was convinced that it had to be someone they knew, or at least that's what he told Gary Nichols.

Nichols wired up the phone on Jim Grund's say-so. He never knew if Susan was even aware of the tap. After a few days, Grund called Nichols and asked him to bring the tape recording of all the calls to the house over that period to him.

Nichols did not even play back the tape himself because he felt it was something personal for Jim Grund and none of his business, so he dropped off the recordings at Grund's law office on Main Street. He never again talked to Jim Grund about the contents of that tape, but Grund's relationship with Susan deteriorated shortly afterwards which clearly implies he heard something highly incriminating on the tape.

Without doubt there were conversations between Susan and some of her male admirers on those tapes. But Jim never revealed if he heard anything that referred to Susan and David. If he ever did play the tapes to any of his friends or colleagues, none of them have ever disclosed that fact. But word of Susan's extramarital activities certainly spread even faster through Peru following the handing over of those tapes to Jim Grund.

In November 1991, relations between Susan and Jimmy Grund were becoming increasingly strained.

Not only was he fed up with the way she often flouted herself in public by wearing outrageously suggestive clothes but, she was by now carrying out a number of secret liaisons with other men. He told her he was particularly concerned about the well-being of the two young children.

To make matters worse, Jacob's real father, Gary Campbell, had come back on the scene, albeit temporarily. Campbell—obviously wracked with guilt about how he allowed the Grunds to get Jacob back—had been making all sorts of promises to Jacob in a series of phone calls and then not bothering to deliver. The result was that the boy was in a highly emotional state most of the time. He was not doing well at school and he was becoming increasingly aggressive at home. Jim had been around long enough to know that the child was being torn apart by his real father's involvement. He didn't want to completely ban Campbell, but would do so if he continued to twist up the little boy's mind.

One day, Jim Grund became so upset by Campbell's attitude that he called and warned him to stay away from Jacob and not to call the boy ever again. Clearly, Jim Grund's only priority was the happiness of Jacob, whom he had long considered to be his own child. Jim could not bear to see the child being pulled backward and forward between parents and genuinely believed that the only way to give Jacob a real chance in life was to keep people like Campbell away from him forever. Jacob adored Jimmy Grund and actually only behaved properly when his stepfather was around, further fueling Susan's built-in resentment toward her fourth husband. In her mind, it seemed they were ganging up on her and there was no way she could allow that to happen.

The spin-off from all this family tension was that Jim was so upset by the wrangling over Jacob that he decided not to attend one of Susan's other sister's weddings. Jimmy Grund was becoming increasingly concerned about his wife's family. He had forgiven her so many things including the near murder of her stepson, but he was beginning to wonder if his marriage to her would prove the most costly mistake of his life.

For her part, Susan was feeling increasingly isolated by Jim's big-buck friends who had grown very dismissive of this pushy woman whom they suspected was not the classy lady she made herself out to be. She had made a niche for herself in the upper echelons of Peru society, but now none of Jim's friends would give her the time of day.

Grund's longtime friend Don Bakehorn, who was co-owner with Jimmy of their favorite bar in town, Shanty Malone's, never forgot going to an Indiana University basketball game with Susan and Jim, who got into an argument over their wills. It seemed that Susan did not like the fact that Jim's law practice partner Don Fern was the administrator of their estates. She was particularly aggrieved about the idea of having to go to Fern to ask for money.

Don Bakehorn was concerned enough by that incident to bring it up with Jimmy Grund a few days later. Jim told his old friend that he would change the will back anytime he chose if he didn't like the way things went with Susan.

Jim also told Don that he didn't believe in prenuptial agreements because "a man should trust his wife or not marry her."

But the tensions between Jimmy and Susan continued. It had got to the point where they argued regularly in public—a bad sign in any relationship.

On a trip to Minnesota for the NCAA playoffs, Susan and Jim really laid into each other when the name of Susan's doctor in Indianapolis came up. It was clear to all their friends present that day that Jimmy Grund was jealous of the doctor and suspected Susan was having an affair with him. Actually, nothing could have been further from the truth. He was the doctor who had made Susan consult an older physician because he was so concerned about the sexual overtures given out by Susan.

Somehow, through all this, Susan continued to keep in contact with her former husband Gary Campbell, despite Jim Grund's decision to blot him out of their lives. No one knows whether they were sleeping together or not, but it seemed as if Campbell was actually trying to get a further loan off the Grunds.

In the midspring of 1992, Susan visited Oklahoma to see her sister Simmy and attend her baby shower. Gary and Susan met for breakfast and talked about Jacob and how he had been progressing in school. Campbell later insisted nothing else happened between them.

Meanwhile, Susan's resentment toward her husband Jim seemed to be increasing virtually on a daily basis. One time, a couple of friends called to drop off some scuba gear they had borrowed and witnessed firsthand the tensions between Susan and Jim when the couple started screaming at one another about some petty point.

In the middle of that particular row, Jim jokingly suggested his wife hire a hitman if she was so cheesed off with him. Susan screamed back that he would probably miss anyhow. Jimmy Grund then said that if someone was going to succeed they should shoot their victim in the eye because of the thin bone structure in that area. Susan Grund looked over at her husband with an intrigued expression on her face. "Really," she thought to herself. "That is *very* interesting."

Around this time, Susan met up with a girlfriend for lunch in Peru and the conversation got around to what Susan was doing workwise, now that her boutique had burnt down.

"My full-time job is setting Jim up good so that if he leaves me, he leaves without anything," came her stone-cold reply. It was a remarkably similar comment to what she had told her senator friend a few months previously. A definite pattern was emerging.

Susan went on to shock another friend by talking in great, proud terms about how she could sexually please men and therefore get everything she wanted. She insisted it was that way with Jim Grund. She clearly made out she had him twisted around her little finger. She also made it clear that she loved sex with other men and would use it for whatever she wanted. Old habits were certainly dying hard for Susan Grund.

In May 1992, Susan started telling some of her closer girlfriends that she was planning to get her and Jimmy's wills changed. She said she wanted to ensure that Tanelle and Jacob got more protection in case either of their parents died.

One friend was astonished when she saw Jimmy and Susan arguing yet again about the contents of their wills at a cookout at a neighbor's home. There was absolutely no attempt on the part of Susan to hide what she was saying.

One of Susan's best friends at this time was Pamela Oglesby. She lived just across the open land that separated each of the huge houses on Summit Drive. Susan and Pamela would regularly call round at each other's houses for coffee and sometimes they would go into town and enjoy a healthy lunch together, usually paid for by Susan out of that generous allowance given to her by Jimmy every month.

Susan proudly boasted to Pamela about her extramarital affairs. She mentioned the accountant, although she insisted that had fizzled out because the sex was not very memorable. Susan also revealed to Pamela that she was hosting a "Wednesday dinner group," which involved businessmen from Logansport. It all sounded incredibly blatant to Pamela, but that was exactly how Susan wanted it to be. She still believed in flaunting her behavior rather than hiding it. The dinner group was supposed to be a gathering of corporate minds where businesspeople could swap ideas. But some suspected it was more like a meat market for Susan to pick and choose whom she wanted to seduce.

There was another man who had had a liaison with Susan at Lake Maxinkuckee, she told Pamela. But she never revealed his name.

Throughout all these brazen confessions of adultery, Susan insisted to her friend Pamela that she had an open marriage, but Pamela had seen the Grunds together as a couple and it was crystal clear to her that Jim didn't like Susan behaving in such a loose manner.

Susan also told Pamela that she was not at all happy with the will Jim had recently redrafted because it still did not have the sort of clauses she believed were essential to Tanelle and Jacob's well-being. She admitted openly challenging Jim to make several changes. Susan kept on saying the will wasn't fair to the children, but the overriding impression was that she was thinking about herself and the possessions she stood to lose. She kept on bringing the subject back around to exactly how much money Jim had.

Susan was careful not to mention her alleged affair with stepson David. Pamela was obviously a little too close to home for her to be told about that alleged relationship.

But Susan's sexual prowess was sometimes overshadowed by the sort of domestic problems most couples can relate to. Jim was fed up with her spending so much money and he told her so one night. He was particularly angry because she had maxxed out her credit cards. Jim got so furious that time he thumped his fists on the table in front of Susan, but she glanced back at him with a totally blank expression. She didn't really care.

Around this time, Susan's glamorous photo once again popped up in the *Peru Daily Tribune*. On this occasion, she was pictured showing eighteen-year-old Kim Vrooman the proper way to walk while on stage during the Miss Miami County contest practice session. The photo was particularly memorable because Susan looked extremely chic and sexy in a short black skirt with black stockings and stiletto heels. Her hair appeared to have been styled especially for the occasion.

Less than two weeks later, she was in the papers again whilst training contestants for the Little Miss Pageant at the Grund home on Summit Drive. There seemed no end to Susan's abilities for self-promotion. Every time she saw her photo in the paper she saw it as yet further evidence of her important role in Peru society.

Susan was also still involved in the reelection campaign for her favorite local senator.

At one particular Republican fund-raiser, Susan even showed up with her friend, the gay choreographer who once had turned down her sexual overtures, and introduced him to everyone there. Many present winced as they watched Susan petting the hand of her male friend. She considered him a great challenge and was still convinced they would have an affair.

That evening, Susan, her friend the choreographer, and Jim Grund, plus a few elite members of Peru's high society, went to an establishment called Homer's for drinks and dancing. Susan never once danced with her husband the whole evening, but she astonished other guests by grinding suggestively up against her gay friend. Susan still felt that the choreographer had thrown down the gauntlet by insisting he was gay. She wanted to prove to herself she could have any man she wanted.

Even more significantly, Susan began having very serious conversations with Jim about them both seeking help from a marriage counselor. She was not keen on the idea, but Jim insisted they could sort out their problems with a little effort on both sides. His eternal optimism was shining through once again. But it was an aspect of his character that would ultimately prove his downfall.

One time, Susan went to Fort Wayne on a shopping trip with a girlfriend and she talked frankly about the problems caused by the large age gap between her and Jim.

Susan moaned yet again about how Jim was always coming home tired and rarely wanted to go out for the evening. She, on the other hand, looked forward to their social life immensely and could not understand or appreciate why he was so tired.

When Susan's friend joked about Jim probably being tired because he was carrying on an affair, Susan snapped back furiously, *"I'd kill Jim if I ever caught him having an affair."*

She even went on to add that during one argument she had told him what she would do if she ever caught him. "I made it quite clear to him that I was serious," she later told her friend.

It was around this time in 1992 that Susan was occasionally spotted out driving with her stepson David on Main Street, Peru. They would be sitting close to each other like a pair of lovestruck teenagers in Susan's car, apparently oblivious to the attention they were provoking in that very small town.

Susan continued to spin her story to certain close friends, telling them that she was having an affair with David and that he was a fantastic lover, "much better than James [Grund]." Susan said it was hard to believe that they were father and son.

When some of Susan's friends tried to persuade her to stop the friendship she became very protective of David.

"He's a really wonderful guy," she purred.

Susan sometimes used her part-time course at law school (paid for by Jimmy Grund, naturally) as an excuse to meet up with David or some of her other male friends.

One of the main bones of contention between Susan and Jim Grund was his ownership and patronage of Shanty Malone's bar. Jim tended to stop by the friendly hostelry most evenings on his way home from his law offices.

Susan found it increasingly irritating that Jim would often find time to drop in and see his drinking buddies, but he was always so tired by the time he got home. Those far-off early days of their marriage when Jim seemed like such a romantic guy appeared to be locked in the past.

However Shanty Malone's actually represented for Jim a refuge from Susan. Her incessant phone calls to the bar when she felt it was time Jim got himself home simply reaffirmed his belief that an evening with his friends, and a few vodka and tonics, was far preferable to a difficult supper for two at the house on Summit Drive.

Jim was encouraged in this belief by most of the regulars at Shanty's—none of whom had any time for Susan. They considered her to be snooty, stuck-up, and dangerous.

Jim Grund was well aware of his wife's bitterness, but he took the attitude that she needed his money, so she was highly unlikely to just get up and leave him.

Sometimes, even Jim was capable of being fairly cruel to his demanding wife. He put her to the ultimate test when he took a woman associate on a business trip to New York City after insisting to Susan that the woman had a legitimate reason for being on the trip.

Susan was livid. Afterwards she heard how nice her husband had been to this woman, although there is absolutely no suggestion that anything of a sexual nature occurred. But that got Susan even more annoyed. She wanted an excuse to pay him back by sleeping with even more men. Either that, or she wanted to give him a deadly ultimatum. At one stage, Susan was so irritated by her husband's apparent fidelity that she started a rumor about Jim having an affair with another woman just to ease her own guilty conscience.

At an Easter gathering in March 1992 of most of Jim's family and friends at the family lakeside cabin on Lake Maxinkuckee, Jim's sister Jane overheard Susan and Jim having a vicious argument about Susan apparently lying about wanting Jim's motor dealership partner Fred (Jane's husband) to repair some of her relatives' cars.

Jim had known nothing about the repairs and became angry at what he saw as an abuse of the business. In the end, Jim got so furious he said he was going to tell Fred to stop repairing Susan's relatives' cars, even at cost price.

Susan stormed out of the cabin and only returned a few hours later to pack her bags and tell Jim, "We're outta here."

When Jim hesitated she screamed at him in a piercing voice, quivering with emotion, and to all those present it seemed very scary.

A few weeks later, Susan telephoned the dealership and talked to Fred Allen. She put on her silkiest Southern-doll voice and insisted that she and Jim had straightened everything out, and Jim would never accuse Susan of lying again or "that will be the end of him."

It was a strange comment to make to your own brother-in-law and it sounded terribly sinister to Fred Allen. He decided there and then that Susan was somebody to keep a close eye on.

# Eight

If Susan was to be believed, her relationship with stepson David was beginning to resemble the mega-famous roles of Mrs. Robinson and the Graduate, played so effectively by Dustin Hoffman and Katharine Ross in the hit movie, *The Graduate*.

During their illicit rendezvous, Susan and David would regularly talk about how he felt toward his father. They clearly did not get on very well, although much of that apparent animosity seemed to be fueled by Jim Grund's generosity towards his pretty, younger wife. David felt frustrated by his father's refusal to pay his son a reasonably sized allowance.

Then, just before Jim's murder, according to Susan, she and her stepson were almost caught in the middle of the act of making love.

David had turned up at the house on Summit for one of his regular, intimate lunches. Just after David arrived, Susan got a call from Jim wanting to know if she would join him for lunch at Shanty Malone's. Su-

119

san told Jim that David was at the house and promised that they would meet Jim down at Shanty's.

But within minutes, according to Susan, she was making love to David in the house. Just then they heard a car approaching. It was Jim turning up in the driveway.

The first either of them knew what was happening was when Susan heard the garage door opening. The two illicit lovers immediately both got up and rushed to get on their clothes. But Susan did not have time to make the bed, something she always did without fail each and every morning.

Susan and David went straight into the dressing room and he just sat down and watched television. At that moment, Jim came in the house. He claimed he'd forgotten something and that was why he had come home unexpectedly. Minutes later, Jim entered the bedroom and noticed the unmade bed. He wanted to know if Susan was getting lazy or if "something was going on."

When he looked at Susan, he knew something was wrong. Susan looked embarrassed and told Jim that they should talk about it later, because she was afraid of what he would do to David if she told him. Somehow Jim bit his tongue and said nothing more about the incident but it was clear he had his suspicions.

At this time, David was in virtually daily contact with his stepmother. It has even been claimed that he was in love with Susan, the unattainable lady whom he originally felt had stolen his father. Although David would later deny that a romantic relationship existed between the two, phone records would show that scores of calls were made between David's home and the house on Summit Drive.

Meanwhile, Susan clearly implied to certain friends

and relatives that she was very much in love with her stepson. Her role as Mrs. Robinson seemed pretty real to many of her friends.

Susan claimed David was regularly turning up at the house on Summit Drive when his father was at work and Susan's two children were at school. On a number of other occasions, she slipped out to the house in the country that he was by then sharing with Suzanne Plunkett. That particular property—on County Road—was just a mile west of State 19 and very easy to access.

On several occasions, Susan employed neighbor Mary Pruitt's son Michael to babysit for Jacob and Tanelle when Jimmy Grund was out of town. Michael never forgot these particular evenings because David Grund was always at the house on Summit Drive when Michael showed up on the doorstep. After giving Michael a briefing on how to look after the children, Susan and David would leave together. Usually, they openly talked about how they were going night-clubbing in Indianapolis. On at least two occasions, David and Susan did not return to the house until the following day. She would always tell Michael to call his mother Mary if there were any problems with the children. She was definitely not going to be contact-able.

Susan's sister Darlene was not in the slightest bit surprised that she contended that the affair with David was continuing. To Darlene, it was typical of her sister. She had enjoyed flings with lots of other men during her four marriages. She had even tried to get fresh with Darlene's husband, but that was the way Susan was in her sister's mind. She wasn't going to change. She always wanted a new man. A new experience. More often than not, once she had done it with the man she got bored of him and wanted to move on to new pastures. But with David, it seemed much more serious.

Susan's stepson and alleged lover was also experiencing the sort of domestic problems with his girlfriend Suzanne Plunkett that can sometimes end in tragedy. The couple had moved in together and were constantly being hounded by Suzanne's ex-husband, the father of her young child, Ryan.

In their desperation to keep the besotted man away, David and Suzanne purchased a 9 mm. semiautomatic handgun.

Jimmy Grund found out about the gun when legal paperwork for a gun permit arrived at 7 Summit Drive, the address David had been using at the time of his application.

Jim Grund was not at all happy about his son having a gun.

"Guns usually create more problems than they solve, David," he told his son.

But David was adamant. He was not going to be intimidated any further by Suzanne's ex-husband.

Jimmy Grund's best friend and Shanty Malone's drinking pal Sgt. Gary Nichols of the Peru Police Department had no doubt Jim's marriage was crumbling well before the spring and summer of 1992.

Despite being the person responsible for that first blind date which initiated Susan and Jim's relationship, Gary considered Susan to be a master manipulator and thought she was becoming increasingly an embarrassment to her husband.

Often Jimmy would pour his heart out to Gary as the two men sat around the table at the end of the bar

happy. Then on one page, only a week or so before that very day, Susan had written that she didn't know whether she wanted to leave her husband or not. She also talked about things getting worse and how she wanted to "crawl up in a nutshell."

The contents of that diary hit young Jacob like a hammer from hell. The very chance that his beloved father and his mother might split up filled him with dread, as it would any young child stumbling upon such a revelation. But what bothered Jacob the most was that he feared it would mean moving away from his new father, the only person in his life who had offered love, care, and attention without wanting anything in return. Jacob had seen how upset kids at school got when their parents split up, but this was even worse because he knew in his heart of hearts that his mother would just replace her latest husband with another man and this time he might not be as kind-hearted as Jimmy Grund.

Not long after that, Jacob managed to talk to his mother alone in the house. He had to know the truth about his parents. Susan told Jacob that she and Jimmy Grund were going to see a marriage counselor. But she said it in such a way that Jacob knew their marriage was probably already over. It filled him with dread.

Susan's mistreatment of children reared its ugly head again in the early months of 1992 when Jimmy's sister Jane's son Brad stayed over one night at the house on Summit Drive. The child told her mother the following day that he had been locked in a darkened room by Susan on his own in the basement of the house. The child—four years old at the time—was so scared of staying in the house with his aunt that Jim Grund had to take the toddler to his office with him the following day until his sister got back from a trip she had taken with her husband.

That incident worried Jimmy Grund a great deal because he had gone to great lengths to give Susan another chance after finding out about the battery of little Tommy in Oklahoma. She had insisted she did not do the things the prosecutors had claimed she did, and that she had never hit a child since.

But the problems with his sister's child made Jimmy start to wonder. He sincerely feared for the safety of any child who might be in her company when she blew a fuse. And he seriously started to question the mental state of the woman he had married.

Jim Grund should have turned to his family to find out what to do next. But he did not want to trouble his elderly mother or father. He felt that if he told them about Susan's troubled background it would only make things worse. It was typical of Jim Grund. He was the type of person who genuinely believed he could sort things out with a minimum of fuss.

Meanwhile, Susan continued to paint a picture for her relatives of her affair with her stepson.

Her mother Nellie had absolutely no doubt they were sleeping together. She believed the relationship was partly built on the fact that David and his father were constantly rowing about his allowance. It had got so bad that every time David wanted money and couldn't get it from Jimmy Grund, he would go to Susan.

Susan put up with it partly because she was attracted to David and partly because she wanted to keep the peace between David and his father, which was fairly bizarre since she claimed she was having illicit sex with David at the time.

Nellie Sanders was up at the house one time when David and Jimmy Grund clashed about money and she heard Jim shout at his son, "You'll not get a dime more out of me!"

Adding to the suspicions about Susan and David's alleged illicit affair was the way they used to treat each other in public. Some of Susan's relatives witnessed them openly touch each other's hands.

One time, Susan even told Nellie that David was "a great lover."

Nellie—naturally very concerned about what her daughter was getting herself into—begged Susan to end the relationship. But she concluded that her daughter was infatuated with her stepson.

In late May 1992, David and his girlfriend Suzanne (later renamed Denise because her other name reminded the Grunds of Susan) were taken on a special vacation by David's mother, Jane, who rented a light aircraft and flew them to Gulf Shores, Alabama, for a week. Halfway through the vacation, Susan and Jim turned up and the fivesome went out for a meal together. Jane was impressed at how well Susan seemed to get on with David compared with a few years earlier when she and Jimmy had thrown the youngster out of the house on Summit Drive because he was so awkward and troublesome.

A few weeks later, at a high-society barbecue in Peru, Miami County Prosecutor Wil Siders was talking to Jimmy Grund about various things when the subject came around to Susan. Grund took a deep breath and then told Siders and another legal colleague, "If I ever die you look at that bitch first. . . ."

His eyes snapped in the direction of Susan, flirting with yet another man across the back yard from where they were standing.

On June 30 that year, Susan made a rare appearance at the cabin on the lake at Maxinkuckee on her own to help David celebrate his twenty-second birthday. She had been extremely instrumental in organizing the event. David's mother Jane was puzzled by this as she had not realized that her ex-husband's second wife and her son were that close.

Jim's sister Jane cooked a special meal for David, but just before they toasted his birthday, Susan made an appalling joke about David and Jane committing incest. It was in especially poor taste since Jane had heard numerous stories about Susan going with other men in Peru.

The room went silent and David coughed and smiled in a brave attempt to break up the tension.

The following day, Jane went out looking for Susan to tell her it was time for lunch. She found her brother's wife sitting alone on the end of the pier. She was deep in thought and did not even hear Jane approaching. Whatever was on her mind seemed to be enormously troubling her.

Around the same time, Susan called a friend in Peru who noticed that when the subject of David was brought up she responded as if he no longer existed. Her affair had obviously come to an end.

Jimmy Grund's parents and his sister were hearing more and more rumors about Susan and David's relationship. Susan had even made a point of telling Jane's husband Fred that she almost always met David for lunch every Friday. Her perverse desire to flaunt every affair, whether they were true or not, was starting to take over this particularly dangerous friendship as well.

Naturally, David played down the rumors and innuendo. He insisted that his girlfriend knew all about the lunches at Summit Drive and was even often with him.

Years later, Connie Grund concluded that David was hated by Susan because he wouldn't sleep with her, although she did concede that the Grund family were concerned at what was happening between him and his stepmother at the time. The truth was that no one actually knew.

July 4, 1992, was a day that Susan Grund would be forced to recall over and over again.

That morning she got up and prepared to go out to the Miami County fairgrounds to help on the stage that had been set up for the 4-H Fair, planned for later the following Monday.

Just before she departed, she got a call from David Grund's girlfriend, Suzanne Plunkett. She asked Susan if she would watch her baby, Ryan, for a bit while she got ready for a Fourth of July dinner she and David were planning to attend later that day.

Susan said she'd try and get by later in the morning and headed off for the fairgrounds.

A couple of hours later she stopped by at David and Suzanne's house to say that she really did not have time to look after the baby as she needed to get home to change for the same event.

David was at the house as well, and he told his stepmother he was feeling lousy because he had spent the previous evening drinking at Shanty Malone's, and he had been up all night vomiting and suffering from an appalling stomach ache. Susan wasn't partic-

ularly sympathetic since that place was the root of all
evil, as far as she was concerned.

David seemed very agitated that day, especially following the threats that had been made to him and
Suzanne by her ex-husband Bobby Olinger. He then
talked to Susan about the gun he had just bought.

Susan stood and looked on disapprovingly. David
was already well aware that both she and his father
were not happy about him owning the weapon.

"There's nothing wrong with owning a gun," insisted David. "There's no reason for you or Dad to be
upset about it."

Then David invited Susan into the bedroom he
shared with his live-in lover and let her handle his
gun. Susan even had baby Ryan in her arms as David
demonstrated the weapon's capabilities.

David referred to how difficult it was to work the
slide on the pistol and he put his arms around Susan
to pull it back sharply. The jolt sent a strange shiver of
excitement through her body.

Just then Suzanne entered the room with a look of
concerned curiosity on her face. Susan quickly broke
the ice.

"You wouldn't shoot anyone would you, Suzanne?"
asked Susan.

"Yes, I would," replied Suzanne coldly.

"But they'd know it was you, Suzanne," replied Susan.

Then Susan looked at David. "How do police trace
guns, anyhow?"

"By the serial numbers on the side of the gun,"
came David Grund's slightly bemused reply.

Susan then asked David who the police would visit
if they traced a gun. He told her in a matter-of-fact

manner that it would be traced back to the registered owner.

The discussion about the gun lasted no more than fifteen minutes. Just before she left, Susan commented on the back door of the house which appeared to be held closed by a boot string. She also seemed unduly concerned about the couple's six-month-old dog they kept in the backyard. Susan departed and David left his home at around 2:00 P.M. to go with Suzanne Plunkett to her parents' home for that July 4 cookout.

Susan headed for the house on Summit Drive where she took a shower and prepared for the same party that she and Jim were due at later.

At 5:00 P.M. Susan and Jim Grund stopped by at the Plunketts' residence in their dealership-loaned Pontiac van as the party was in full swing. With them were Jacob, Tanelle, and Susan's nephew Paul, visiting once again from Oklahoma. The children swam in the Plunketts' pool, everyone ate and chatted, and then the Grunds went home.

After arriving back at their house, Susan and Jim prepared for a more adult party they had been invited to later that evening at the home of Roger Timme, the construction expert who built and designed the house on Summit Drive.

But then Susan decided it would be inappropriate to leave all three youngsters on their own at the house, so Jim went to the party alone.

Susan claimed she got a message shortly after Jim Grund left about a missing curtain that was needed for the 4-H show the following Monday, so she took Tanelle with her and dashed off to sort it out.

A number of Jimmy's friends had shown up at the party at Roger Timme's expecting to meet the handsome gay choreographer who had stunned Susan by refusing to have sex with her the previous year. The story of her rejection had reached almost legendary proportions among the elite of Peru and they were all dying to meet the man who turned Susan down. Unfortunately, he did not show up either.

At 7:30 P.M., David Grund received a phone call at the Plunketts' from his stepmother asking David if he and Suzanne were going to watch the fireworks that night at Maconaquah Park. David told Susan he was still feeling sick and was not going to bother, so he would most likely stay at the Plunketts' for the rest of the evening.

At around 8:00 P.M. Susan, Tanelle, and a school pal of hers came back to the house for a mini fireworks display before they planned to head off for the main event at 9:00 P.M.

When David got back home about 10:00 P.M. that night he immediately noticed something was wrong. A drape had been knocked down. At first, he thought maybe the wind had done it, but then he walked into the bedroom and saw the TV flipped down on the floor. Then he moved around the bed and saw the gun had been stolen. He immediately called the Indiana State Police.

Trooper Earle McCullough was on the scene within a short time. He was puzzled. Nothing in the house but the gun had been touched by the burglar. It was clear the intruder wanted only one thing.

That break-in was the final straw for David and Suzanne. They moved out of the isolated house in the countryside to an apartment on Main Street, in Peru, within days. They suspected the burglary might be something to do with Suzanne's ex-husband, even though they knew he was in jail at the time.

The theft of David's gun obviously rested uneasily on Susan's conscience. Her close friend and neighbor Pamela Ogelsby never forgot how Susan had an unnerving habit of suddenly bringing up the subject of the missing gun. Usually it was completely out of context with what they had been talking about previously.

One time, about two weeks after the theft, Pamela was talking to her friend about her own impending divorce and her sick parents when Susan butted in, "I hope nothing happens with that gun that was stolen." It was never far from her mind.

On Sunday, July 11, 1992, Jim, Susan, and six other couples went on a flat-bottomed boat trip together down the Eel River.

There were problems from the outset because none of the others wanted to be in a boat with Susan, and in the end she was made to sit between Jim and his law partner Don Fern.

As the boats were floating downriver alongside each other, Susan threw what appeared to be a ball of mud at Dr. John Crawshaw, one of her husband's best friends. Inside the mud was a rock and it nearly knocked the doctor unconscious. No one ever discovered what had made Susan so angry at Crawshaw or why she should have gone to such extraordinary lengths to hurt him.

Some members of Peru's high society believe that Susan was angry at the doctor because he had refused to sleep with her a few weeks earlier following a drunken party.

It seemed that if Susan didn't get what she wanted someone always had to pay. . . .

# Nine

In July 1992, Susan's son Jacob became so upset by an argument he overheard between his parents that a few days later he asked his mother outright if she was planning to divorce Jimmy Grund.

"Yes," came the reply. But Susan did not elaborate and never made reference to it again.

On another night earlier that month, Jimmy and his wisecracking pal Gary Nichols got so drunk down at Shanty Malone's that they demolished the front door of the house on Summit Drive when Jim found he had forgotten his keys.

Susan was furious at what happened. She thought that Jim's behavior was hardly that of an upstanding citizen of the local community and, in any case, what if the neighbors heard what had happened? It would do her reputation around town no good whatsoever. She never once asked if either Jim or his friend had hurt himself in the process of smashing down the front door.

Susan harbored a lot of resentment over that incident. She just would not stop going on about it to Jim. In the end, he agreed to let her buy an $1800 front door made of the finest wood. It was a ridiculously expensive item, but Jim just wanted Susan to shut up about the incident and he knew her well enough to know he could buy himself out of her bad books with relative ease.

The house on Summit had become the ultimate evidence of money's importance to Susan when she had stomped into Jim's office years earlier and demanded that Jim buy the land and have the property built. When he demurred, she threw a tantrum, screaming and yelling until he finally agreed.

In more recent years he might have managed to keep a slightly tighter rein on Susan's spending. Or at least he tried. Despite his remonstrations to curb her extravagances, Susan usually found a way around her husband's prohibitions. She had not hesitated to forge his signature on a check when she needed more money for her fashion business and she would not hesitate to do that again, if necessary.

On July 17, just a couple of days before Jimmy, Susan, and the kids planned to depart for a summer vacation to Alaska, a very significant meeting took place at Jimmy Grund's law offices on Main Street, Peru.

In front of Jimmy's legal secretary Diana Hough, Susan signed up her share of a new joint will drawn up by Jimmy Grund. Their previous will had been drawn up on October 31, 1986. Diana Hough never forgot how surprised she was that Susan insisted on all sorts of changes, nearly all of which would either benefit her or her children in the event of Jimmy's death. But the most memorable clause concerned her best-known obsession—the quality cars she insisted were provided to her by Fred Allen from the dealership business he co-owned with her husband.

The will clearly mentioned, "an agreement that my wife, Susan A. Grund, be provided a demonstration vehicle for transportation on a like basis as she has been provided throughout my lifetime. I request that should Fred J. and Jane A. Allen exercise this option (to buy the business outright after Grund's death), they will agree to provide her with a vehicle similar to those provided in years past throughout her lifetime or until such time as she remarries, whichever event should occur first."

*Susan had thought of everything in the event of her husband's death.*

Shortly after this, Jim Grund secretly visited another lawyer colleague in Peru and warned him that on his return from vacation in Alaska he would want to begin divorce proceedings against Susan. He planned to file a petition the week after his return. Grund told his friend he wanted Susan out of his life forever. He was tired of working incredibly long hours to keep her in jewels and designer clothes, only to discover that she was trying to hop into bed with just about every rich and powerful man in the county. Whether he suspected Susan of being in a relationship with David has never been thoroughly established.

Jim Grund told Susan of his divorce plans when they were both on vacation with Tanelle and Jacob in Alaska. He also told her that she wouldn't get custody of the kids, the house, or any of his money. Clearly, Jim had found out something so devastating about their marriage that he wanted it to end immediately. There was also the matter of those tape recorded telephone conversations from a year earlier. The contents of them had deeply disturbed Jim, but he had chosen not to act upon them at the time.

The trip to Alaska was partly a reconnaissance trip for Jim to seek out new fishing grounds so he could return with his pals for one of his regular trips. But he also felt it was time, despite the divorce plans, that he and Susan and the children actually enjoyed a break together away from Peru and all the wagging tongues and vicious gossip.

Susan was not very keen on going to Alaska. She presumed it would be dirty, uncomfortable, and extremely boring. Susan also may well have been particularly annoyed about the trip because it delayed her plans, which had got under way the moment she apparently stole that gun from her stepson. No doubt Jimmy's divorce announcement was the final straw.

The truth was finally dawning on Susan that her luxurious life as the wife of a successful lawyer was drawing to a close and she had no immediate wealthy candidates with which to replace him.

In the early hours of Saturday, August 1, 1992, Susan, Jim, and the kids arrived from their Alaska trip exhausted after a delayed return flight. That afternoon, they were due at an office picnic at Jim's father's lakeside cabin at Culver on Maxinkuckee Lake, but they were so tired they turned up late. Jim's partner Don Fern ended up organizing most of the party together with the numerous secretaries from the law firm the two men co-owned on Main Street, Peru.

Don Fern noticed that Jimmy Grund seemed tired but elated by his vacation with Susan and the two children. He kept making a point of saying sorry for not being able to get round earlier to help with the cookout. In contrast, Susan seemed muted and only managed a thin-lipped smile each time she was asked if she had enjoyed a pleasant vacation in Alaska.

Don Fern hardly got a chance to talk to his buddy Jim Grund as he and Susan were amongst the first to leave the gathering. They apologized profusely about their early departure, but they were exhausted after that long trip back from Alaska.

Early on Monday, August 3, 1992, at 8:00 A.M. sharp, Jim Grund left his house on Summit and turned up at his office. Before departing, he told Susan he had a lot of appointments that day and would not be back home until quite late.

By all accounts, Jim was in good spirits. He bumped into Miami Circuit Court Administrator Scotty Webster and spent several minutes discussing his trip to Alaska and what a great place it was.

"Scotty, you have to go there sometime," enthused Jim Grund.

Webster never forgot how happy Jim had seemed on that day because it was unusual for the former prosecutor to be so expressive; normally he was a pretty laid-back character. It was as if a weight had been lifted from his shoulders. He kept on about looking forward to the future—a future he wanted without Susan. Jim then strolled off for an appointment in Wabash.

Susan's first chore of that day was to drop off little Tanelle for tennis practice at the Thursh Courts on East 3rd Street in Peru at 10:30 A.M. Susan then went down the street to her mother's shabby, rundown house opposite where her sister Darlene lived, on the wrong side of town.

Susan then visited a nearby grocery store with her mother's shopping list and purchased the week's

Susan at age eighteen (*left*) and at a high school reunion,
showing her fondness for money (*right*).
(*Courtesy of Mary Heltzel*)

The ramshackle house in Peru, Indiana, where Susan grew
up. (*Author's Collection*)

Tommy Whited with his father, Susan's third husband, Tom Whited. (*Courtesy of Lester Suenram*)

Susan's only son, Jacob, and Tommy. (*Courtesy of Lester Suenram*)

The house on Rushing Road, Oklahoma, where Susan almost battered Tommy to death.
(*Author's Collection*)

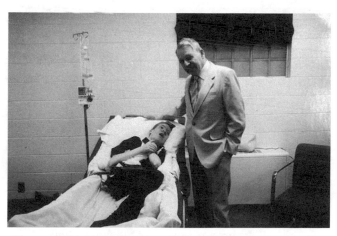

Tommy with his caring grandfather, Lester Suenram, after Susan's horrendous attacks.
(*Courtesy of Lester Suenram*)

Susan and Jim Grund at their Florida wedding with baby
Tanelle. (*Courtesy of Connie Grund*)

Susan in a sexy pose for a photo she insisted Jim keep with
him all the time. (*Courtesy of the Grund family*)

Jim on vacation during his first marriage with daughter Jama (*left*), wife Jane, and son David. (*Courtesy of Jane Grund*)

The Grund clan (*top row*) Jane, Fred, Jeff, Jim, (*middle row*) David, Jane, Jama, (*bottom row*) James A., and Connie (holding baby). (*Courtesy of Jane Grund*)

David Grund striking a happy pose with step-mother Susan, who later testified they had been lovers. (*Courtesy of Jane Grund*)

The semi-automatic weapon used in the murder of Jim Grund. (*Courtesy of Peru Police Department*)

The vast mansion on Summit Drive, where Jim Grund
lived and died. (*Author's Collection*)

The family plot in
Peru where Jim
Grund is buried,
complete with an
aircraft insignia
on the gravestone.
(*Author's
Collection*)

Detective Jay Einhorn (*left*), chief investigator into the child abuse charges against Susan, and Don Deason (*right*), the Assistant DA who prosecuted Susan—and then was asked out on a date by her! (*Author's Collection*)

Detective Sergeant Gary Nichols, Jim Grund's best friend and one of the lead investigators into his murder. (*Author's Collection*)

shopping for her. At 12:11 P.M., Susan headed off to the D.M.V. offices where she bought licence plates for the camper she recently had purchased for her mother.

Lunch was spent with Tanelle and her mother Nellie in town. Then they headed over to a nearby campsite where the newly-purchased camper was parked. Susan noticed that it had been damaged by recent rain so the two women closely inspected it to see what repairs would be needed.

At around noon on nearby Main Street, Don Fern saw Jim Grund as he walked down the sidewalk near their office. He seemed in a good mood.

At those same law offices on Main at around 3:00 P.M., Jim's brother-in-law and car dealership partner Fred Allen called in to ask Jim to trade cars with him that evening when they met for dinner at the Fireside Inn in nearby Logansport. Jim seemed in good spirits, but there was a little edge in his voice when it came to the subject of Susan and what her next dealership car should be.

"Make sure you don't give Susan anything too nice, Fred. She's been naughty and that '88 Camaro will do just fine."

At around the same time, Susan drove home and picked up Jacob from the house before driving him to her sister Darlene's house at 412 East 3rd St. Susan then drove herself and her mother to Logansport, just fifteen miles away to do some more shopping.

Back in Peru, Jimmy Grund was making his daily appearance at Shanty Malone's. His close friend Dr. John Crawshaw bumped into him at the bar and the lawyer regaled his friend with tales about the family's adventures in the barren northern state of Alaska. He also mentioned that Susan had been a pain during the vacation, but did not expand on exactly why. Jimmy then had time to have a quick drink with his good friends Gary Nichols, attorney Pat Roberts, and Dick Sims.

In Logansport, Susan and her mother purchased gifts and clothes and Susan dropped her mother off at her own house at around 6:00 P.M. On arrival at her mother's tatty home, Susan found a message on Nellie's answering machine from Jim Grund, asking her to call him at home.

Jim Grund informed his wife that she would have to switch cars that evening because his partner and brother-in-law Fred Allen had sold the grey Buick she had been driving around for the previous month. Susan was annoyed with Jim because it meant she would have to remove all the gifts and purchases she had made earlier in the day. But Jim was adamant. He had always warned Susan that the cars she drove were strictly on loan from the dealership and that they had saved many thousands of dollars in vehicle depreciation and car insurance charges through this arrangement.

At around 7:00 P.M., Jim turned up at Nellie Sanders's house in his regular brown Toyota convertible. Darlene was spraying weed killer over the front porch of her mother's house as he bounded up the steps, obviously in a bit of a hurry. He had promised Fred he would take the car to a dinner meeting they had arranged at the Fireside restaurant in Logansport and he was already running late. Jim Grund even went to the trouble of calling Fred at the Fireside to say he would be late for their seven o'clock dinner date because he had only just located Susan and managed to swap cars.

After Jim left with the grey Buick, Susan helped her

mother with her hair before taking Jacob and his cousin Steven Worden (Darlene's child) out to stay overnight at the new camper that evening. As part of that plan, Susan drove Jacob, Steven, and Steven's girlfriend, Patty Ann Seifert, to her house where Susan dropped her off. Susan then went home with Jacob to pick up his sleeping bag and other overnight belongings.

Over in Logansport, Jim turned up for dinner with his brother-in-law at about 7:40 P.M. He was wearing the same suit and tie he had been wearing all day. Jimmy Grund seemed delighted that his brother-in-law had brought along a black Camaro for Susan. He knew that she would consider it more scuzzy than usual. In fact, he told Fred he couldn't have cared less if Susan had the worst car on the lot.

"She's been bad and she doesn't deserve any better," said Jim coldly. Whatever had happened between them was obviously grating on Jim Grund.

At 9:30 P.M., Jim Grund arrived back home from his dinner appointment with Fred Allen and proudly showed his wife the black Camaro he had traded with Fred. Susan was not impressed; she considered the Camaro to be a redneck's car, the sort of thing her own relatives might drive, but certainly unsuitable for a lady about town. That car made Susan very angry, although she still managed begrudgingly to make her husband some cheese and crackers, which Jim Grund took with him as he walked into their ground floor bedroom and started watching the Olympics on their big-screen TV.

By the time Susan departed a few minutes later with Jacob for the campsite, she was back to fuming about her husband's choice of cars. How could he do this to me? she thought. I will be the laughing stock of Peru if I'm seen driving round town in a Camaro.

Susan was convinced that Jim had made certain she was given a car she would hate. She saw it as a sign that he was serious about getting a divorce. Susan was deeply concerned because she did not want her marriage to end yet. After all, she hadn't found a suitable replacement for Jim and she was well aware that if a divorce went ahead then her extramarital behavior definitely would be thrown back in her face and cited as a cause. She'd be left penniless. In Susan's mind, that was a completely unacceptable scenario. She started to consider her only other option. A plan was taking form in her mind. She had already laid the groundwork by stealing David's gun. Now she might actually have to go ahead with that last option.

Before going to the campground that evening, Susan headed back to Darlene's house to pick up her sister's son Steven. She later claimed it was just after ten when she arrived because the local TV news was on and she recognized anchor Clyde Lee, whom she had met some years previously. Throughout the entire evening, she never once mentioned to her mother or sister that Jim had planned to divorce her.

It was between 10:30 and 11:00 P.M. when she finally made it to the campsite with the boys. But on arrival she realized she had completely forgotten the key to the next-door camper, which had all the snacks and food inside it. Susan had also forgotten to bring drinks for the boys and had to return to her mother's to get the drinks and the key to that other camper. It had just started raining lightly and she almost slipped over on the loose wet bricks that lined the pathway to her mother's rundown house as she rushed in to get the goodies.

Susan also picked up Tanelle and her cousin Andrea from her mother's house across the street and took them with her back to the campsite before they headed off to Summit Drive. She later told investigators that she unlocked the other camper and removed the food for the boys and stayed another thirty minutes while she settled them in. The children even managed to watch the 11:00 P.M. *Married . . . With Children* comedy show as Susan told the boys how to work everything in the camper.

"Make sure you stay in, don't cause any trouble," lectured Susan to the boys before departing.

Then Susan headed off back to her mother's house after realizing she had forgotten to pick up her dog, Sugar. But Nellie Sanders shouted out the window at her daughter that it was too late, she was asleep, and she should come back the following day for the dog.

"Make sure you've locked the house up good and tight, Momma," Susan told Nellie. "And don't come out till morning. . . ."

It was a strange thing to say, but Nellie thought nothing more of it until many months later.

Susan then headed for Summit Drive with the girls, arriving home at around midnight. The only reason they had kept quiet throughout the tedious runaround was because they were transfixed by a Nintendo game they were playing in the back of the car.

Within minutes of getting to the house, the little girls gathered up their sleeping bags and pillows from Tanelle's upstairs bedroom and moved down to the basement where they were going to sleep in the cozy den. Susan made sure they cleaned their teeth before they settled down.

"Can I go kiss Daddy good night?" Tanelle asked.

Susan hesitated for a moment after hearing her

daughter's words. Then she replied, "You'll have to give Daddy a kiss in the morning because he's already asleep, sweetheart."

It was shortly after this that Susan turned off the rest of the lights in the house and retired to the bedroom only to discover Jim Grund's body, or so she later told investigators.

No one has ever conclusively established exactly what happened in the few minutes leading up to Jim Grund's death, but one thing seems certain: Susan aimed her stepson's gun directly into her husband's eye, just as she had been advised by him to do all those months earlier.

# Ten

Among the platoon of investigators that swarmed to Jim and Susan Grund's house as soon as it was discovered that a murder had taken place were three men who would play prominent roles in events that followed: county prosecutor Wil Siders, Jim's best friend and Peru Police Department Sgt. Gary Nichols, and Robert Brinson, a tough Vietnam vet who would direct the investigation on the part of the Indiana State Police.

With their greater resources, it was decided that the ISP should run the investigation into the murder of Jimmy Grund. The inquiry was coordinated through Det. Sgt. Bob Land with Indiana State Police Investigator Brinson as the lead detective. He was to be assisted throughout by Trooper Investigator Gary Boyles and technician Dean Marks.

Bob Brinson, forty-six, tended to wear his state trooper's badge with real pride. As a master trooper investigator, he had worked on numerous homicides throughout Miami County. His stern, straight-faced appearance disguised a dry wit and humor that come with fifteen years of police experience, not to mention two terms in Vietnam as a naval CB, building everything from roads to hangars to huts, often as enemy gunfire rained down on him.

Brinson immediately jumped into the nitty-gritty that accompanies any homicide investigation, chronicling details of the scene and trying to keep out of the way of the team of crime scene specialists who were turned loose after Jimmy Grund was officially declared dead. While Brinson moved methodically through the house, sketching the layout of the rooms and noting anything that seemed out of place, technicians took pictures, dusted for prints, and catalogued samples of material that might prove valuable later, both in narrowing down the list of suspects and helping to convict the killer or killers.

Back at Summit Drive, at around 3:00 A.M., Susan Grund tried for the second time to phone attorney and family friend Jim Boyles. This time he was in and told Susan to inform her sister that neither of them should give any more help to the investigators.

In the living room area, Brinson was appalled to overhear two officers discussing their theories as to who had committed the killing. When county prosecutor Wil Siders—waiting outside the house—suggested interviewing certain people there on the spot, Brinson intervened. This was his investigation and no one—however rich and powerful—was going to prevent him from doing his job in a fair-minded manner. That was the final straw; Brinson herded everyone out of the house and off the property. Some were none too happy about it, but, Brinson explained, he had a job to do. Brinson had the unenviable task of actually proving that someone had murdered Jimmy Grund. He wanted to stay unbiased, but it was difficult in this hostile atmosphere. Certain people already had made up their own minds who the killer was.

Brinson himself already suspected that the bullet which killed Jimmy Grund came from his own son's gun. Rumors about Susan and David had been around Peru for quite some time. All sorts of possible scenarios were going through Bob Brinson's mind. What was David's role? It looked a little ominous at that early stage in the investigation. And if David was not involved then why did the killer steal his gun and use it to commit murder? And if Susan was the chief suspect then why would she be trying to frame her stepson?

At 4:00 A.M.—just a few hours after her husband's murder—Susan Grund agreed to meet Bob Brinson at the Indiana State Police Post in Peru, despite her lawyer's advice against it. Her sister Darlene and her husband George drove Susan in George's pickup truck. The meeting was, in the words of Brinson, the beginning of the "cat and mouse" games.

Susan seemed pale and nervous, but not particularly grief stricken, as Brinson sat her down in the small interview room, switched on the tape recorder that stood on the table between them, and carefully read through her Miranda rights.

Brinson began with some pretty basic questioning.

"Who d'you think might be a suspect in the death of your husband, Mrs. Grund?" Bob Brinson had a way of putting things that made everything sound perfectly ordinary. The tone of his questioning was more akin to asking someone if she took two sugars or one in her coffee.

Susan did not seem the slightest bit perturbed. "I don't know, Bob."

Brinson grimaced when she started calling him by his first name as she had been doing back at the house. It made him feel uneasy. Then Susan blatantly panned her eyes down from Brinson's face to that special below-the-belt zone, only to snap her eyes upward again. What was she playing at?

Then she did it again. This time there was no mistaking it. That seductive glance. The licking of her lips. Then she subtly thrust her breasts forward just enough for Brinson to notice. He knew that if he had smiled back she would have happily laid out on that table there and then and encouraged him to make love to her. How could she behave in this way just a few hours after her husband had been shot dead in their bedroom?

Bob Brinson resisted Susan with relative ease. After his long and varied experience as a state trooper, he wasn't about to throw away his career in one stupid moment. This was the calling card of the arch manipulator. She was trying to flirt with him to water down his interrogation of her.

Just then she clasped the investigator's hand in hers as he stood alongside her. Brinson tensed up instantly and pulled his hand away.

This was not the behavior of an honest victim, thought Bob Brinson.

Then he noticed she was once again staring at his groin area. She wanted him to see her doing it. Susan had spent her life seducing men and Investigator Brinson was going to become her next conquest unless he was very careful.

Eventually, Brinson's initial inner tension relaxed and he made a conscious decision to play along with her seductive games. It was obviously going to be the only way to get her to open up about what had happened.

He once again started questioning Susan on a very basic level, asking her things like her children's names, ages, her family background. He was trying to soften her up because what he really wanted to know was whether there had been a time during the previous evening when she had been alone at the house on Summit Drive.

Every now and again, Susan shed a few tears, but to Brinson's expert eye they seemed far from genuine. She kept saying she had no idea who had killed her husband. In Brinson's opinion, she was giving an Oscar-winning performance. But he wasn't finished yet.

Susan went on to tell Brinson all about the obscene phone calls she said she had received and how she contacted the telephone company, who had made a report to the Indiana State Police. Susan also claimed that Jimmy Grund had heard some of these obscene calls as well. (Brinson actually traced the police report that had been filed as case #16–5834 on March 15, 1991.)

Brinson then changed tactics and began asking Susan about her husband's will. There was no point in beating about the bush, he thought to himself. She knew perfectly well why he had brought her in, so why not get down to basics?

"Has your husband made any new wills recently, Mrs. Grund?"

At that moment, Bob Brinson could have sworn he saw her lip curl and her tongue run seductively across the lower part of her mouth.

"I left all that to Jimmy," she purred. "Apart from going to his office and signing on the dotted line."

Susan was supremely cool at this stage, even though it was absolutely crystal clear that Brinson suspected her of being involved in her husband's murder. She even admitted that Jim and she had signed a new will on July 17, 1992, less than a month before the homicide. She insisted that she had gotten him to change his will because of their vacation to Alaska.

"Was anyone else present when you signed the will?"

Susan said that Jim Grund's legal secretary Diane Hough had been present throughout, but she repeated her claim that she could not remember the details of that meeting.

Susan then switched topics and began speaking in emotive terms about that last vacation, how good it had been for the kids to be with their father. She started sobbing. Then she went on, only to stop again within minutes. Then more sobbing.

Brinson was already well aware of that other break-in two years earlier, which he suspected had been stage-managed by Susan in order to make an illegal insurance claim. He also wondered whether it had been a dry run for the actual murder of Jim Grund.

He was especially keen to find out more about the carefully balanced seminude photograph of Susan that was found so conveniently positioned on a drawer following the alleged burglary and killing of Jimmy Grund. He asked her if she regularly posed for such photographs for her husband.

Another seductive smile curled onto Susan's lips as she nonchalantly recalled to Brinson that she estimated between thirty and forty such photographs had been taken. Brinson was a bit surprised—after all, he was interviewing the wife of one of Peru's most prominent citizens.

Just before winding up the interview, Bob Brinson decided to ask Susan the most obvious question of all. "Can you guess why anyone would murder your husband?"

Susan did not hesitate in her reply.

"I cannot."

"Is there anything you want to add to this tape that you think we ought to know at this point?"

"No."

*The strangest aspect of that interview from Bob Brinson's point of view was that Susan Grund had repeated, almost word for word, what she had told him just after that burglary at her home in 1990. The only difference this time was that her husband had been murdered.*

Bob Brinson was never actually contacted by Susan Grund again following that interview. That, in itself, made him very suspicious of her role in Jim's death. Usually, relatives of slain people were on his back within days if not hours of such a killing. They would pester him and demand all his attention. They always wanted to know what was happening, who the suspects were. They tended to want answers, even more than the investigators themselves. But not Susan Grund.

With many of Peru's top notch citizens awakened in their beds the previous night with the news of Jimmy Grund's murder, an account of his killing rapidly reached the town newspaper, the *Peru Daily Tribune*.

ATTORNEY FOUND SHOT TO DEATH was enough to grab the attention of any curious members of the community.

Investigators were at first naturally reluctant to provide the press with many details. Indiana State Police Sgt. Bob Land even refused to say whether there had been signs of a struggle or forced entry at the house on Summit Drive.

Up at the property, a row of brown and tan police cruisers outside the house contrasted sharply with the serenity of the wealthy area. Residents in the exclusive neighborhood were dismayed by the news of Jimmy Grund's death.

"He was always friendly and seemed like a nice person," said neighbor Thea Hoppes in a statement that could have referred to any of the hundreds of violent deaths that occur each week across the United States.

None of the residents who lived on the estate recalled hearing gunshots the previous evening.

Peru school superintendent Tom McKaig, who had worked alongside Jim Grund in his capacity as an attorney for the Peru School Board, was just as stunned. He told reporters, "I knew him well on a professional basis and that's probably why I'm sort of sitting here in my own shock. Jim dealt with a variety of things from negotiations to policy matters to personnel matters, and he always handled them all in an exceptional manner."

Also quoted in the *Peru Daily Tribune* August 4 report of the murder was Wil Siders, president of the Miami County Bar Association and the county's chief prosecuting attorney.

"I think anyone that ever worked with him would give him all the respect as an attorney," said Siders. "Members of the bar association lost a good member of the bar and a good friend. I feel very deeply for his family."

On the day of the murder, police had to get a subpoena from the Honorable Judge Bruce Embrey ordering the Dukes Memorial Hospital to produce the taped telephone conversation between Susan Grund and the ambulance service. Sgt. Kenneth Roland served the subpoena to the hospital administrator and immediately had the tape transcribed. Wil Siders believed it might prove to be crucial evidence at a later date.

Wil Siders never at any stage felt his close proximity to the Grund family would in any way hinder his abilities as a prosecuting attorney. Yet he obviously was seriously upset about the killing of his friend and colleague.

Judge Embrey, who was to later be involved in the initial stages of the arrest—and charging of an eventual suspect—was also quoted in that same article in the *Peru Daily Tribune*. He had been to the house within hours of Jimmy Grund's death, along with Wil Siders.

Judge Embrey said, "It's like losing a family member. The whole thing is just a terrible shock."

He had never forgotten how, a few years earlier, Jimmy Grund had been piloting a light plane they had been traveling in to Bloomington for an Indiana University ball game. The engine had started spluttering at ten thousand feet and they had to make an emergency landing in a field. Judge Embrey decided never to fly in a small plane again.

Embrey and Wil Siders had spoken at length during their visit to the house on Summit Drive, just a short time after the shooting of Jimmy Grund. Both played a prominent role in bringing the killer to justice, despite their close connections to the family of the victim.

Investigator Bob Brinson was very concerned about

the presence of both the judge and Siders in the case. He felt that they were too personally involved.

Brinson felt the same way about Jimmy Grund's good friend Peru Police Sgt. Gary Nichols. At the start of the investigation, he found Nichols to be very biased against Susan and it created endless difficulties. Brinson fully appreciated how hard it must have been for Nichols to separate his personal and professional views when such a close friend was a murder victim, but he found Nichols's involvement in the case irritating. Brinson felt that some of the law enforcement officials who knew Jimmy Grund were trying to tell him how to do his job, not to mention the fact that they all believed they could solve the murder in a split second, if given the chance.

Nichols believed—rightly or wrongly—that Brinson was deliberately choosing to ignore his advice in those early stages of the homicide inquiry. He considered Brinson to be overconfident of solving the case quickly. Gary Nichols had known Susan Grund for almost ten years and in his opinion she was going to be the toughest nut of all to crack. He genuinely believed that Brinson would need all the help he could get. Also, Nichols felt a twinge of guilt. After all, he had been the one who first introduced Jim to Susan.

His own feelings of responsibility manifested themselves in a near obsession with Susan's guilt. His best friend had been murdered by the woman whom he had suggested to Jim for a blind date. Nichols had always been more aware of Susan's darker side than Jim, who had been prepared to give her the benefit of the doubt during the early years of their marriage.

Gary Nichols's emotional feelings about what had happened to Jim Grund were driving him into the investigation whether other officials liked it or not. He was not going to stay out of it until Susan was brought to justice.

The day after the killing, reporters began appearing at the house on Summit Drive in dribs and drabs— many of them had trouble even finding the isolated property and spent hours asking round the neighborhood for directions.

Down at Shanty Malone's on South Broadway, regulars were exchanging consoling hugs and collecting money for flowers.

As news of the murder of Jimmy Grund spread across the town, it sent shockwaves through the tightly-knit community.

Hours after the murder, a sign was hung on the door of the law offices of Fern, Grund, and Grund. It read, "Office closed due to the death of James Grund."

Workers at the office were naturally upset by the news. One of them, Christian Sands, summed up the situation when he said that Jimmy Grund's impact on his career would stay with him for the rest of his life. "He took me under his wing. I don't know why exactly. I guess I was lucky."

The day after her husband's appalling slaying in the house on Summit, Susan Grund moved back into the property. Investigators and others in Peru were surprised that a grieving widow should return so quickly to the scene of such an awful crime.

Susan also moved her children Tanelle and Jacob back into the vast house. All three of them stayed in the basement of the property. It deeply disturbed the youngsters that they were expected to sleep in the house, but Susan could not stand the mess and clutter of her sister's and mother's homes on 3rd Street, Peru.

A few days after moving back in, little Jacob told one family friend, "I don't understand why Mommy got us back in the house where Daddy got killed." He was clearly shaken by the situation.

Helicopters buzzing overhead probably didn't help, either.

Less than twenty-four hours after the killing, Gary Nichols broke all the rules by flying above the house on Summit Drive in a helicopter he was piloting on behalf of the county for another investigation. The other case involved a homicide where it was believed the victim had been buried in the backyard of a house, and Nichols and another technician were ordered to fly over that property and see if there were signs of a disturbance in the backyard using a highly complex infrared camera that was sensitive to within a tenth of a degree. Nichols was only one of six people in the state of Indiana certified to make such infrared searches.

However, on the way back from the real reason for his flight that evening, Nichols decided to go and take a look at his old pal Jimmy Grund's house, in the UH1-style helicopter on loan from the local National Guard. The aircraft was very similar to the types of choppers used to ferry troops to front lines during the Vietnam War.

Nichols openly intended the constant whirling of those massive rotors as he flew just above treetop level across the open countryside near the Grund mansion to "psychologically freak out" Susan, if nothing else. And since he was up there anyhow, it made sense to give it a whirl.

As Nichols hovered hundreds of feet above the property, he pointed the infrared camera in the direction of the backyard of the house to see if there were any signs of fresh marks in the soil. But there was nothing. After ten minutes of psychological warfare he swept away into the night. Gary Nichols felt that at least he had done that for his old friend Jimmy Grund, if nothing else.

A few days after Grund's murder, Susan put a call into Nichols at the Peru Police Department. She did not even mention the killing. She just wanted to know if he would be able to copy a photo of Jim that she wanted to use at his funeral. She did not even ask if the police had any suspects for her husband's killing.

Initially, stories swept round Peru claiming that Jimmy Grund had been murdered by a vengeful former client or someone he had convicted during his days as a young, ambitious county prosecutor between 1978 and 1982.

Within three days of his death, investigators were openly saying they did not think that was likely.

County prosecutor Wil Siders was especially adamant and made a point of telling local reporters, "I don't think this had anything to do with Jim as a prosecutor."

To add to the initial confusion about the case, Indiana State Police were swamped with calls from the public, some of them claiming that both Jimmy and Susan had lovers, others that a contract had been put out on Jimmy.

Investigators found that the constant supply of rumors were making their inquiries even more difficult because they were having to follow up every lead to see if they had any validity and that was stretching their resources to the absolute limit.

Meanwhile Miami County Coroner Dr. Daniel Roberts was predicting that it would be at least two to three weeks before the full results of the autopsy on Jimmy Grund's body could be released.

A few days after Grund's death, his sister Jane decided it was time to tell her five-year-old son Brad what had happened to his "uncle Jimmy." This was the same little boy who had been made by Susan to sleep in a darkened room on his own at Summit Drive, then ended up spending the day at Jim Grund's office because he was too scared to stay at the house alone with Susan.

Moments after Jane had tried to sensitively inform the boy of his uncle's murder, Brad started screaming and began kicking the dashboard of the car they were driving in at the time. He did not stop screaming and kicking until they had covered the entire ten-mile journey home. His mother had to start taking him to counseling shortly afterwards.

# Eleven

In a town the size of Peru, the murder of a prominent lawyer was big news. Jimmy Grund's death was
the lead item in the local media from the day he was
killed and for many weeks afterwards. But in the early
stages of the investigation, Brinson and his team of
detectives did not want to make any foregone conclusions. It was only when they began delving into Susan
Grund's past that the picture of an all-American family unit started to fall out of focus. When they looked
beyond the obvious and started examining the background they came away with a whole new perspective.

A lot of things about this case were starting to
greatly trouble the ISP investigator. He had recognized the shell casing lying on the carpet in the bedroom as belonging to a 9 mm. automatic pistol. The
moment he saw it he reckoned it had to be from the
gun that was reported stolen from David Grund a
month earlier.

That particular case #16–6768 had stuck in Brinson's mind because it seemed so bizarre that the thief

who stole the gun had touched nothing else during the alleged break-in on July 4, 1992. With this in mind, Indiana State Police Trooper Gary Boyles was dispatched to interview David Grund straight after his father's death. He told the investigator that his stepmother Susan had arrived at his apartment on Main Street the day of the "theft" and he had shown her his pistol.

Boyles and his colleague, crime technician Marks, then asked David if he could supply them with any practice casings or slugs he might have, for comparison with the casing found at Summit Drive following the shooting of Jimmy Grund. David Grund told them there were almost certainly some at the house in the country where he had been living until the spate of recent death threats by his girlfriend's ex-husband.

Boyles then asked David about his precise movements on the night of the murder. There was no getting away from the fact that he was a possible suspect.

David insisted he was watching television. Boyles probed further and it emerged he had been watching the same programs as Boyles. The investigator closely questioned him about the story lines of each show. David seemed to know them all inside out. Boyles was impressed. He never once wondered why David should have such an incredibly detailed knowledge of every single twist and turn of at least three major television programs.

Within the week, Indiana State Police laboratory examiners at their building in Lowell had matched the shell casings and slugs taken from David's gun to that found in the sofa behind Jimmy Grund's exit wound to the head. The ISP lab also examined blood and hair samples.

Other interesting aspects of the case began to

emerge over the days following the news of Jim Grund's murder spreading throughout Miami County. Sgt. Bob Lilly of the county sheriff's department contacted Bob Brinson to say that during the recent Miami County 4-H fair he had talked to Susan Grund and she had informed him about the threatening phone calls she received the previous year. Susan had been most concerned about how quickly the police would get to the family house on Summit Drive if called out on an emergency. Perhaps this had been an excuse for a dry run?

On the day after the murder, a search warrant was served on the Peru Trust Bank for the safety deposit box #1126 in Jimmy Grund's name. However, no items of jewelry were found and bank records indicated the safety deposit box was purchased by Jim Grund on February 2, 1989. Jimmy had actually only been near the box three times since purchasing it. Various papers were found in the box plus four life insurance policies worth a modest total of $61,770. The beneficiary was Jim Grund's daughter Jama for three of them, but no beneficiary was named for the last one of $20,000.

A few hours later, Brinson and his unit of investigators interviewed Jimmy Grund's law practice partner Don Fern, who advised officers that he and Jim had a "buy-sell agreement" dated May 6, 1991. Attached to the agreement was a $150,000 life insurance policy. Fern stated that Jim Grund and he recently had invested some money into remodeling, and additional office space had been taken on loan. The life insurance policy was purchased to protect the other partner in the event one of them died unexpectedly.

Don Fern also supplied the Indiana state troopers with a copy of Jimmy Grund's first will dated October

31, 1986, and the more recent version dated July 17, 1992.

Within twenty-four hours of the murder, Brinson and his investigators had the sensitive task of interviewing Susan's daughter, Tanelle. The little girl's story tallied with most of what her mother had told Brinson in the early hours of the morning of the previous day except for one significant incident. She said she remembered her mother dropping off at their home in the late afternoon and rushing into the house to get something and then emerging with it hidden carefully behind her back. She then put that object in the trunk of the car. Brinson could only surmise it was the murder weapon.

Publicly, at least, the investigation into the murder of Jimmy Grund seemed to be drawing a complete blank. Newspaper headlines like INVESTIGATORS FIND FEW CLUES IN SHOOTING implied that Grund's killer was a mystery assailant.

Capt. Tim Hunter of the Miami County Sheriff's Department insisted to reporters, "There's not a whole lot to go on."

Even one of Bob Brinson's colleagues at the Peru post of the Indiana State Police was quoted as saying, "There are no firm suspects at this time. We don't want to speculate on things and mislead you."

The day after this—August 6—another subpoena was obtained. This time it was for the telephone records of the house at Summit Drive. In addition to this, prosecutor Wil Siders and other officials ordered that a tap be installed on the home phone line.

Sgt. Gary Nichols made the appropriate connections and started monitoring. A daily computer update was made available from that time forward for a total of sixty days.

As news of the murder spread statewide all sorts of other interested parties began to come forward with information that would eventually prove invaluable to the investigators.

Attorney Patrick Roberts told police he had been a close friend of the Grunds for many years and he had heard Susan and a neighbor up at Summit Drive discussing whether it was a good idea to own a gun. Susan had come out against the idea and told her friend that she disapproved of how another neighbor was living with a man who kept a gun. That neighbor's live-in lover overheard Susan say a few weeks before the killing, "Well, I hope nothing ever comes up about that gun being stolen at David's house."

This was a major breakthrough for Brinson because it was the first time a witness had mentioned David's gun and Susan in the same breath.

Meanwhile Roberts was insisting to investigators that he thought Susan was having an affair with her doctor in Logansport. When interviewed later, the doctor fervently denied this and police entirely believed him. But then they discovered the accountant.

Then Brinson stumbled upon a complete bombshell—and it almost put him totally off the scent. Susan had been involved in a bizarre relationship with a fifteen-year-old schoolboy.

The youth—who attended the local MaConaquah School—had a complete obsession with Susan and was even known to have stalked her around town. He kept photographs of her in his locker at school and the boy had been continually getting in trouble for bad behavior at school. The boy's sister even claimed that he kept other, near-pornographic photos of Susan under his mattress at home. The daughter told their father that the boy had told her "he was going to kill James Grund."

At first, Bob Brinson was astonished about the story of the love-obsessed boy and he seriously considered him a prime suspect in the killing of Jimmy Grund. Officers immediately traced his family home in Peru and rushed round to apprehend their "killer" only to discover he was already in a state boys' school for persistent offenders.

On August 7, Brinson and his investigators contacted Susan's third husband, Thomas Whited, in Oklahoma City. What he told them did more than anything to convince the Indiana State Police investigators that Susan was their most likely suspect.

Whited initially explained that he had only been married to Susan for less than a year. When Bob Brinson asked what went wrong with the marriage, there was a long pause on the other end of the phone line. Whited coughed uncomfortably and then went on to reveal the full, disturbing story of little Tommy's beatings at the hands of his cruel and twisted stepmother.

Brinson confirmed Whited's claims when he did a criminal record search and discovered that Susan had indeed been given five years' probation for the attack on Tommy. When Brinson asked Whited what condition his son was in now, he got a brief reply: "He is a vegetable."

But under further questioning, Whited also admitted reaching an agreement with Jimmy Grund wherein the lawyer released Whited of any legal responsibilities for Tanell Grund in exchange for Whited giving Susan $25,000 for a trust fund for her daughter by Whited.

Whited also revealed to investigators that little Tommy's paternal grandfather Lester Suenram of Oklahoma City had filed a $45,000 damage suit naming the Baptist Hospital where the youngster was taken when he was injured the first time, because the attack was not reported to the police. The case was eventually settled out of court.

Thomas Whited also described Susan as "the world's greatest liar." He even told investigators how, despite having a prenuptial agreement with Susan, she still continued to get on his back about setting up a will to provide for her if anything should happen to him.

Shortly after interviewing Whited, the Indiana State Police post received a call from Jimmy Grund's father, James A. Grund, saying he had also located the Oklahoma City police report on the battering of little Tommy and Susan's subsequent arrest. Everyone in Peru, it seemed, wanted to play the role of homicide investigator.

Brinson noted that Oklahoma City Det. J. M. Einhorn, who had been in charge of the investigation into Susan, said she had lied about several aspects of that case, even to the point of calling the family doctor and suggesting that her brother had got into a fight and had the symptoms later found to be consistent with the injuries to Tommy. Einhorn even stated in his report he had contacted the brother to establish that he had never suffered from such injuries.

Susan Grund was a confirmed liar . . . but did she murder her husband?

# Twelve

The day before Jimmy Grund's funeral, Susan appeared at the funeral home and insisted that her husband wanted to be buried in Macey, a little town north of Peru where his grandparents on his father's side were buried. She also claimed that Jimmy had specifically requested that his brother Jeff not attend the funeral.

Jim's parents, Connie and James, were furious. They had a family plot at the Mount Hope Cemetery in Peru, and that was where their son was going to be buried. But Susan was so adamant she insisted on holding a meeting with her husband's grown-up children, David and Jama, to discuss the issue. What made it all the more bizarre was that by this time many people—including the entire Grund clan—definitely believed that Susan had murdered her own husband earlier that week. Investigators had begged all concerned not to confront Susan, in case she tried to flee the state.

Finally, it was agreed that Jimmy Grund could be

buried in the family plot just so long as Susan could have her ashes buried with him when she died. The Grunds agreed to her demands with absolutely no intention of ever carrying them out. They simply wanted to make sure the funeral service went off without any embarrassing scenes caused by "grieving widow" Susan.

On August 8, the day of the funeral, one of Susan's neighbors from Summit Drive walked over to the Grund residence and talked to Susan outside the house.

"They'll never solve the murder of Jim because they never could figure out who burglarized the house," Susan told her neighbor in a remarkably businesslike manner. The neighbor decided there and then that Susan knew who had pulled the trigger.

At 11:00 A.M. that morning, family, friends, and members of the community paid their respects to Jimmy Grund when Miami Circuit Judge Bruce Embrey called a packed courtroom to session for a memorial service conducted by the Miami County Bar Association. It was standing room only.

Local attorneys and those from neighboring counties presented resolutions with expressions of regret for losing Grund, but also out of gratitude for having known him.

Judge Embrey fought back tears as he told the packed assembly, "I'm going to remember a smiling Jim Grund who always had a kind and upbeat word."

Then he said bitterly, "I look forward to the day when this veil of anger and frustration and feeling of pain lifts and we can all remember those good moments."

Susan Grund watched from the front of the courtroom, looking stunning in a tight-fitting black dress and subtle, matching pumps. Her hair gracefully combed back into a bob, she could not help outshining every other woman present, even though virtually no one was prepared to talk to her.

Judge Embrey also read a letter from Superior Judge Garratt Palmer, who couldn't get to the service. Palmer wrote that Grund would be greatly missed in the court and community.

"A 'friend of the court' in the finest sense of that term will be lost," he wrote.

Lawyer Pat Roberts represented the county bar association by reminding the audience of Grund's keen ability as a lawyer. Roberts also recalled Jimmy Grund on a personal basis, talking of his generosity and after-hours friendship.

The courtroom then went completely quiet as Jimmy's father, James A. Grund, got up to address his son's accomplishments.

Grund told the story of a day when his son, with whom he shared an office, came in and talked about how easy it is to complain about the legal profession. Grund told his father there were too many arguments between attorneys.

Then he looked at his father and said, "I just wanted to let you know how much I appreciate practicing with you."

At the end of the memorial service, a very small number of people offered their condolences to Susan who hugged each one in turn, making sure she saved her most emotive hug for when a photographer from the *Peru Daily Tribune* pressed his motor drive button.

Jimmy Grund's actual funeral service at 2:00 P.M. that afternoon was a very large affair with an eighty-car procession. It took eight pallbearers to carry the casket because Jim Grund had insisted on being buried in a Sequoia wood coffin and, as one pallbearer explained, "It weighed a helluva lot." As the graveside service was conducted by the Rev. J. Robert Clark at Mount Hope Cemetery, the sun shone brilliantly.

Then just before Jim Grund's casket was lowered into the ground, a tiny black rain cloud stopped overhead and deposited a brief shower on all the mourners.

Suddenly there was a clinking from the coffin. A few of those present smiled gently. Gary Nichols had put two bottles of Jim's favorite vodka and tonic in the casket as a farewell gift. Above them, the small, dark rain cloud continued pouring rain drops on all the mourners.

"That was Jimmy pissing on us," said one of the pallbearers looking up at that small, black cloud in the sky. Most of his closest friends managed a smile.

For Jimmy Grund's close buddy Nichols, the whole event took on an eerie significance because he was burying his friend on his own birthday. He was also deeply disturbed because he and most of Peru's ruling class were convinced the killer was standing just three feet from the casket. There had even been talk just before the ceremony of planting a bug at the graveside, in case Susan made some sort of confession in her moment of grief.

The only good thing that came out of Jimmy Grund's death in the eyes of all those hardened friends and colleagues was that Susan began referring to Grund as "Jimmy" after his murder. It was a name she steadfastly refused to use when he was alive.

Just a few yards from the site where Jimmy Grund was laid to rest was a semicircular arch. To the left of that was a large conelike stone that read COLE. There are several round stones, like rolled up pillows. This was the burial spot of Cole Porter and his wife Linda, Peru's two most famous residents.

After Jimmy Grund had been laid to rest, one of the mourners described Susan as being as stiff as a board without a tear in her eyes.

Susan seemed determined to keep up appearances despite the Grunds' extraordinary snub of her at the funeral of her murdered husband. She even went to great lengths to send a card to every single person who sent her a letter of condolence. The card read:

> *Just when friends are needed*
> *You find them always near;*
> *Just when shadows are darkened,*
> *Their comforting words you hear.*
>                     *Thank you*

The cards were all signed Susan, Jacob, and Tanelle Grund.

After the funeral, Susan and the Grunds even held rival wakes at their respective homes. No more than ten people went to the house on Summit Drive. Susan pretended to her sister-in-law Jane that dozens of people had attended.

At Susan's party, her brother suggested that he purchase Jim's Toyota for a knockdown price. Susan, well aware that all her money was frozen, accepted a miserly offer and sold the car before her husband's body was even cold in his grave.

The day after the funeral, Bob Brinson stepped up his investigation, safe in the knowledge that now that Jimmy Grund had been laid to rest the townsfolk would be expecting him to double his efforts to apprehend Grund's killer.

Brinson made arrangements with Susan and her mother Nellie to meet with him at the Indiana State Police post in Peru. She had agreed to take a polygraph. Nellie showed up exactly on time at 9:00 A.M. But then one of Susan's sisters, Rita Saylors, telephoned at about 9:15 A.M. to say that Susan wasn't feeling very well and wouldn't be able to come in for the interview. Rita explained that she had been staying with her sister at the house on Summit Drive since the murder.

Bob Brinson was very irritated by Susan crying off like that. He had talked with her the previous day about doing a polygraph test and she had seemed more than willing to participate. Now she was playing shy and it worried Brinson. He had a feeling she was going to make a run for it if he was not careful—and he knew how much flak he would get from Wil Siders and all the rest of the town if that happened.

Brinson got into his blue Ford Taurus and went straight to the Grund residence. Susan's sister Rita came to the door in a very protective manner, hardly opening it wide enough for him to see her entire face. Brinson tried to be gentle, but firm. He had an arrangement with Susan Grund and she had let him down. She had to take that polygraph test.

Just then, Rita exploded into an emotional outburst. She accused Brinson of holding a witch-hunt for her sister and she was very upset that anyone would even dare to suspect her beloved sister of murder. Brinson was taken aback; the last thing he wanted was his suspicions out in the open. He believed the best way to deal with his chief suspect was not to accuse her outright at this stage simply because he knew he did not have enough evidence to pin it on her in any case.

Brinson pleaded with Rita to hear him out. He had specially scheduled a polygraph and the technician was waiting down at the state police post in town.

"That polygraph would help prove your sister's innocence," explained Bob Brinson patiently.

At that comment, Rita slowed down and thought for a moment. It did seem to make sense. She suggested that Brinson wait until the first of the week and then contact Susan again about rescheduling the polygraph and holding another interview.

He pulled out a business card with the following information: Indiana State Police, Bob Brinson, 473–6666.

"Tell her to call me if she needs anything."

Bob Brinson was irritated. He had not got what he wanted, although it could have been worse. She might have thrown him out and refused outright to even take a test or come for another interview. But he knew full well that the longer she had to think about things the more likely she was to get her story absolutely airtight, and that was bad news for his investigation.

Brinson was trying to divide the investigation into three important segments. He believed that once he had the answer to each of these points he would solve the entire case. They were:

1. The gun.
2. Susan's extramarital affairs/her credibility.
3. Insurance claims.

Brinson knew that Susan's ultimate aim must have been to snare a high roller like the senator she had been hanging around with in recent months. He knew that her boutique had burnt down in highly suspicious circumstances and he knew that she was obsessed with never going back to the *wrong* side of the tracks.

That same day, two of Brinson's colleagues carefully drove the route given by Susan and her family members as the route they took on the night of Jimmy Grund's murder. The mileage was recorded from Nellie Sanders residence at 419 East 3rd to the reservation campgrounds. The time was recorded as the investigators drove at the posted speed limits.

The route to the Grund residence at Summit Drive from the campgrounds also was measured and timed via both the river road and the Wayne Street bridge in town. A return route using Bus 31 across the Kelly Avenue bridge and through downtown Peru using Main Street to the Sanders's residence at 419 East 3rd also was measured and timed. The times and measurements recorded were very relevant to checking out the various accounts of what had happened that night:

| | |
|---|---|
| 419 East 3rd Street to R.V. | 2.8 miles/ 5.0 min. |
| R.V. to 7 Summit Drive (Wayne Street Bridge) | 6.0 miles/ 9.5 min. |
| 7 Summit Drive to 419 East 3rd Street | 3.1 miles/ 6.5 min. |

Bob Brinson was intrigued. During her earlier interrogation just after Jim Grund's murder, *Susan had claimed that it took her almost double the time to cover the same trips.*

Two days later, on August 10, lawyer Nick Thiros contacted Brinson and his unit to inform them that he had been officially retained by Susan Grund. Thiros, from the Merriville area of Indiana, did not exactly surprise Bob Brinson when he informed the trooper that his client would not submit to a polygraph or any further interviews by the police.

Coincidentally, on that same day, Brinson's colleague, Sgt. Ken Roland notified the trooper that he had met with a confidential informant who had described knowledge of a so-called plot to kill Jimmy Grund as early as six weeks before his actual murder. The source insisted that Susan's former husband Gary Campbell had been telling friends that he was going to get a gun to kill Jim Grund or that someone was going to get a gun for him.

The details of these claims were a little sketchy, but the idea was apparently that Campbell would make sure he had an airtight alibi for the night of the killing. Sergeant Roland's mystery informant even told him that he himself had been so concerned by the alleged plot that he made an appointment at Grund's office to warn him of the murder scheme. But when he got to the office, he discovered that the Grunds were on vacation in Alaska.

Bob Brinson was so taken aback by this entirely new development that he felt an obligation to thoroughly check it out. A member of his unit even visited Jimmy Grund's law offices and obtained the appointment log which clearly recorded that the informant had called on July 23 at 12:45 P.M. and had scheduled an appointment on August 10 at 2:00 P.M. The investigator's ears pricked up at this news. Maybe there was something in the claim after all.

Then Jim Grund's legal secretary Diane Hough pointed out that the source's call had been about a legal settlement Jim Grund was handling for her. No mention had been made about death threats at the time and surely if the danger was so imminent the informant would have said something.

Brinson was feeling a little confused by this stage. He did not want to ignore such a significant claim, but it did not look particularly reliable.

The following day his unit interviewed Michelle Harshman, one of Gary Campbell's ex-wives. She denied all knowledge of a plot to kill Jim Grund and she insisted that she had not—as the informant had claimed—overheard any conversation about guns or killing by her ex-husband. She even told investigators that she had not seen or heard from Campbell since their marriage broke up in 1989. The tip was another dead end.

Indiana State Police Investigator Brinson was about to wind up the interview when Michelle had an afterthought that she felt obliged to share with the officer.

"I know Susan's nephew Paul and he told me that he caught Susan in bed with Gary at Gary's house in Oklahoma City in 1991," said Michelle in a very casual, matter-of-fact way.

The investigator looked up, but said nothing in the hope that Michelle would continue. She did.

"Paul also told me he caught Susan naked in bed with some guy at his mother, Rita Saylor's [Susan's sister] house in Kokomo." Michelle then provided more details of Susan's alleged extramarital activities.

Bob Brinson's biggest problem through the initial stages of the Grund murder investigation was that he had the greatest difficulty keeping anything confidential because anyone who was anyone in Peru believed they had a right to access his case file. Brinson had no way of controlling the leaks. It was a logistical nightmare for the hard-working investigator.

In any case, Brinson was back to square one and his main suspect was still Susan Grund.

But that didn't stop her contacting a company called Kemper Insurance about a $250,000 life insurance policy on Jimmy. She was very anxious about how quickly a payment could be made to her following her husband's death.

# Thirteen

On August 12, 1992, just one week after the murder of his father, David Grund agreed to take a polygraph test for Indiana State Police Investigator Bob Brinson. It was a controversial move by the state trooper who was only too aware of the Grund family influence in Peru and the fact that everyone in town had tried and convicted Susan Grund in their own minds, and found her guilty of first-degree murder.

But Brinson was a stubborn son of a gun and he did not like the fact that everyone was walking around Peru treating Susan's guilt as a foregone conclusion. He was extremely concerned about the relationship between Susan Grund and her stepson David. He had discovered that she was a regular visitor to the boy's apartment and before that, to his house in the countryside outside town. He also had discovered that Susan was not averse to using her body for her own sexual satisfaction, and a lot more besides. Brinson had his suspicions that maybe David and Susan had a thing going and perhaps they had devised the entire "theft" of the gun as a stunt to confuse investigators when it came to the subsequent murder of Jimmy Grund. And even if that was not the case, there had to be a reason why Susan had used her stepson's gun as the murder weapon. Maybe she had tried to enlist David and he had turned her down? Then, she had decided to keep the gun to make sure that David would not testify against her for fear he would be implicated in the killing? Bob Brinson knew full well that David was a crucial player in his investigation.

Despite the fact that all his investigations pointed to Susan as the sole killer of her husband, Bob Brinson wondered whether Jim Grund had been murdered as part of some larger conspiracy, a plot involving another family member other than Susan, perhaps Grund's son. Within forty-eight hours, Brinson would discard this theory entirely, but at the time it seemed to make sense.

David Grund was in deep shock about his father's killing. But as a law student, he knew that his involvement—after all it was his gun that was used to shoot Jimmy Grund—was questionable on the surface, although none of that mattered because he knew he had the whole town behind him. The only person they wanted to see up there in the dock was Susan.

However, Bob Brinson and his Indiana State Police unit still had questions about David's involvement. There was no getting away from that fact that his gun was the murder weapon. And they had received calls from Peru residents insisting that David and Susan *did* have an affair.

Initially, Bob Brinson had been impressed by Trooper Investigator Boyles' account of his earlier meeting with David just after his father's murder. But David's apparently photographic memory of the TV programs he'd watched on the night of the killing of his father did bother Brinson.

However, David willingly visited the Indiana State Police Post in Peru, and allowed trooper Sgt. Mark James to give him a polygraph test. Bob Brinson—still disappointed about his failure to get Susan to submit to a similar test—was very anxious to find out if David was somehow involved. Some of the other town officials were outraged that he should even vaguely suspect David, but Brinson was determined not to be swayed by the high and mighty of Peru's closely knit upper class residents.

David was understandably nervous when he showed up at the ISP's Peru post. He went through a brief pretest interview, during which he was told the nature of the questions he would be asked during the polygraph.

Then Sergeant James placed two pneumotubes on his upper and lower chest. Next followed a blood pressure cuff before wires were linked to two of his fingertips to measure his eventual perspiration during questioning. The theory behind polygraphs is that they measure the fear of detection in a subject. Experts claim that when a subject lies his or her body goes into what they call flight mode and that is picked up on the graph linked up to those wires.

When Sgt. James began asking some of his ten, carefully-formulated questions to David, his body went almost instantaneously into flight mode. Over the following hour and a half, David took at least three separate tests, during which he was asked the same set of questions. Between each test the heavily perspiring law student was given a breather so that his blood pressure did not get too high. The polygraph machine measured David's temperature, blood pressure, perspiration, and breathing throughout the questioning. A straight line on the polygraph told the examiner that he might not be answering truthfully.

The specific responses of David to the polygraph have never been revealed. There was a virtual cloak of secrecy thrown around his involvement in the case and many of the town's most powerful figures went to great lengths to prevent anything other than the barest details of that polygraph test ever being revealed.

Bob Brinson's carefully documented report of the case's initial stages only mentions the following, hidden in the middle of a wordy thirty-six page report:

On 8-12-92 David Grund was given a polygraph examination by Sgt. Mark James. David failed the polygraph. It was suspected that David may have problems with feelings that his stolen gun was used to kill his father James Grund. A second polygraph was scheduled later after David has time to recover from the emotions on his father's death.

The report does not mention the specific questions that David was asked for the polygraph test. It does not detail any of his actual responses at the time. And there is absolutely no reference to the results of any further tests. Certain officials in Peru admitted two years later that no such follow up polygraph test ever took place.

Undoubtedly, David would have been asked whether he was involved in his father's murder and the earlier theft of the gun from his home. His failure at the time left the question of his involvement open to conjecture. And ISP investigators even gently interrogated him further following his failure on the polygraph machine, as they would do with anyone who was a murder suspect and failed. Details of that interrogation are also very hard to come by.

Information about David's polygraph test was kept completely out of the local newspapers, who gave every other aspect of the case saturation coverage for the first three months following the killing.

While polygraphs are by no means conclusive, they are used regularly by corporations across the United States for prospective employees and it is estimated they have a ninety-five percent success rate in relation to establishing whether a subject is lying or not.

The whole question of David Grund's relationship with his stepmother was pivotal to the entire inquiry. Jimmy Grund's good friend and colleague Gary Nichols put it in less than flattering terms when asked if he thought that David had had an affair with Susan.

"Let's put it this way; blow jobs don't count, do they?"

Gary Nichols insisted afterwards that he did not mean to imply that David was involved in a physical relationship with Susan, but it does make one wonder.

Nichols—who was probably closer to the entire scenario than any other person in Peru—openly admitted that David Grund was "not the best boy in town at that stage."

He went on, "Like father like son. David drives a Toyota, Jimmy drove a Toyota. Jimmy married Susan, David's girlfriend is a girl called Suzanne, although she now calls herself Denise."

Nichols believed that David and his father were very much alike and, if that was the case, then Jimmy Grund's son could be capable of doing *anything*.

To further confuse the situation, investigators were

given a deposition by David's girlfriend's ex-husband during which he insisted that David had been seen at a local bowling alley with his gun days after he had reported it stolen.

If true, this would imply that David was involved in the death of his father. But investigators and later, Susan's defense attorneys, were never able to find any other witnesses to back those claims. And given the ex-husband's possible bias, they were not credited.

Susan's mother Nellie to this day believes her daughter and insists that Susan and David were lovers. She never forgot the giveaway signs that her daughter and her stepson were getting close, the touches, the smiles.

"David was red-hot for Susan. I could tell. It was all so obvious," Nellie later insisted.

Most significantly, prosecutor Wil Siders admitted the following in February 1995: "If there is any part of Jimmy in his own son then I could believe it [that David was having an affair with Susan]. But I don't care if David screwed her or not."

Other friends of the couple believe that Susan did have an affair with David, but that it ended a few months before the murder and she was so angry with her stepson that she deliberately tried to frame him for the killing. They are convinced that David did not want his father to know about the relationship and he got Susan to agree to keep it secret. But when she saw David together with his girlfriend Suzanne, she got insanely jealous.

Interestingly, Bob Brinson did manage to persuade David's girlfriend Suzanne Plunkett to take a polygraph and she passed with flying colors, providing David with an alibi for his movements on the night Jimmy Grund was murdered.

It is absolutely clear that Bob Brinson and his unit of investigators did suspect David Grund of being involved in his father's murder up until that point in their inquiries. Why the finger of suspicion was lifted after the results of these polygraphs became known to certain law enforcement officials has never been fully explained.

In the middle of all this, Brinson found himself with the frustrating task of knowing more about the case than he could ever prove. A lot of anonymous callers had contacted the Peru post of the Indiana State Police, making suggestions about others being involved in the murder of Jimmy Grund. But when Brinson tried to persuade the callers to identify themselves, the line always went dead.

What really concerned Bob Brinson was that it was becoming increasingly clear that a lot of people knew much more than they were admitting. But the cloak of secrecy that surrounded the activities of certain members of Peru's tightly-knit upper class was proving impenetrable.

Two days later, Brinson's unit was once again approached by their earlier informant who had insisted Gary Campbell was involved in Jim Grund's murder. The source was indignant that the troopers appeared not to believe her. But Sergeant Roland, who had conducted the original interview, noticed that his informant was not so sure of the actual details of her claims. It seemed almost as if she had been pushed into going back to the investigators by someone. Bob Brinson had his suspicions who that person might be.

That same day, August 14, investigators checked the records at the Miami County Jail to find out if the ex-husband of Suzanne Plunkett (David Grund's girlfriend) was in custody on the night of the murder.

Records clearly indicated that he had been in jail from June 26 on charges of intimidation filed by David Grund which meant he could not have been involved in the theft of the gun. He was still in jail on those same charges when Jimmy Grund was killed.

In Peru itself, people were starting to ask why Susan Grund had not yet been arrested. Her supposed guilt was a poorly kept secret. Pressure was mounting on the investigators for a fast result.

This was especially frustrating for the Indiana State Police officials involved in the inquiry because they were trying to remain as impartial as possible, despite the personal links that just about everyone had with the case.

On August 18, Indiana State Police District Commander Lt. Carlos Pettiford was obliged to make a statement about the fact that detectives from his Peru post had been working on the case seven days a week since the homicide. "They have put in enormous hours and we plan to continue until we apprehend someone or until we have more leads to go on. This is a priority case," insisted Lt. Pettiford.

Meanwhile, one of Susan's closest friends telephoned the house on Summit Drive to offer her condolences.

"Wouldn't it be terrible never to know who killed Jim?" asked the friend.

The line went silent. Only Susan's uneven breathing could be heard. Then she spoke, "What do you mean?"

"I mean, to never know who did it," replied the friend.

Susan immediately changed the subject and began talking about the family's vacation in Alaska.

Two weeks after Jimmy Grund's murder, Susan and

the children moved out of the house on Summit Drive and headed for a house her aunt had rented for her in Vincennes, Indiana, where many of her relatives lived.

Thousands of feet overhead, the FBI were piloting a light aircraft that swooped overhead the house as she departed. The investigators had no idea where Susan was heading. In fact, they feared she might be trying to slip out of the country in a bid to avoid justice.

Susan never even noticed the air surveillance team, mainly because the Air Force base near Peru was usually so busy that the distant buzz of a plane was not even worth thinking about.

Susan's son Jacob was her only passenger as she had already sent Tanelle ahead with her sister. In the car, Susan behaved very strangely towards her young son, repeatedly saying to him that she didn't want to live any longer because she thought the police believed she had murdered her husband. One can only wonder what long-term effect this must have had on the child.

On the ground, a surveillance team car occupied by four investigators including prosecutor Wil Siders, Sgt. Gary Nichols, and Bob Brinson kept a safe distance from Susan. They watched her through night-vision sight binoculars.

Susan spotted shadows on the ground and once she got on the freeway she pushed her foot to the floor and topped speeds of ninety miles per hour. She managed to lose the investigators just outside Indianapolis. Nichols and Siders were infuriated. It seemed as if she was always able to get one step ahead. They knew they were dealing with a very clever lady.

Luckily, the tiny, single-engine aircraft that also had been shadowing Susan since she left Peru remained glued to her car. It stayed with her until she got to her mother's house in Vincennes.

Afterwards, Gary Nichols and his colleagues agreed that they should have put a "bird-dog"—a homing device—on Susan's car.

By the time she got to Vincennes, Susan knew she had been followed, but was pretty sure she had shaken them off her tail. However, the constant presence of policemen was making her very nervous. She was convinced her phones in Summit Drive had been bugged by investigators. Susan also knew full well that her husband's great friend Gary Nichols regularly worked surveillance jobs for the FBI and DEA. She feared that Nichols would do everything in his power to try and prove she had killed Jimmy.

After a few days in Vincennes, Susan befriended a member of her local church called Thomas Wolf. Although she emphatically denied any sexual liaison with Wolf it is clear that Susan confided a great deal in him. Wolf himself later claimed that Susan even confessed to him that she was hiding the gun that killed Jimmy Grund in the old church parsonage.

On August 17, Brinson's ISP unit of investigators interviewed Jimmy Grund's longtime business partner and old friend, Don Bakehorn. Bakehorn owned the American Stationary Company in Peru, as well as being a co-owner with Jimmy of Shanty Malone's. Bakehorn was very anxious to aid police in their hunt for Jimmy Grund's killer and offered them all the help he could. But despite his assistance no new leads came out of the interview.

The following day, Gary Nichols suggested that Bob Brinson contact Florida businessman Jack Vetter to set up a scheme that might just help them smoke out Susan. They believed Vetter's close personal ties to

Susan and Jim would make him the perfect person to try and trick a confession out of Susan. He had even witnessed their wedding on his boat nearly ten years earlier. Vetter assured investigators he would be more than happy to allow them to wire him up so as to record any subsequent meeting with her.

Bob Brinson fully realized that this was not going to be the simple open-and-shut scene he thought it would be when he first got involved. With only a small investigating unit available, Brinson regularly called on the FBI in Indianapolis for assistance with surveillance on Susan and others. There was also the matter of interviewing some of Susan's relatives in Columbia, South Carolina, something that was out of ISP jurisdiction.

The surveillance requirements of the case also meant calling on the help of Sgt. Gary Nichols, who just happened to be an expert snoop as well as Jimmy Grund's best friend.

Initially, Bob Brinson was not particularly happy about bringing on board someone with such close personal ties to the victim, but he needed all the help he could muster, and Nichols's reputation as a superb surveillance operative was second to none. Brinson was pleasantly surprised by Gary Nichols's attitude. He seemed much more open-minded and dedicated to legitimately solving the case than he had been just after Grund's murder.

In fact, Gary Nichols had never stopped being determined to bring Susan to justice, but after his initial burst of outrage following Jim's murder, he started to realize that it would take an enormous team effort to crack the case and everyone needed to pull together. Nichols also had immense sympathy for Bob Brinson because what had appeared an open-and-shut case was now proving to be an extremely difficult investigation because there was simply not enough lawful evidence to prove Susan had murdered her husband.

Gary Nichols was asked to supply audio tape equipment and a transmitter to record conversations between Florida businessman Vetter and Susan Grund. And then he set to work wiring Jack Vetter.

Nichols's dual role as Jimmy Grund's best friend and a very active investigator in the murder case was still questionable, but entirely understandable. He was hungry to find Jim's killer and he had the expertise that might well come in very useful as the net closed in around Susan Grund.

Nichols—a twenty-year police department vet—did not shy away from letting the whole world know his feelings about Susan. "She was the Antichrist of Peru and Jimmy was God," he would tell anyone who would listen.

Nichols was so upset by the murder of Jimmy Grund that he did not even like to glance at the scene-of-the-crime photos that showed his great friend lifeless and bloody with a ghastly death mask expression across his face as he sat slumped on that couch in the bedroom of the house on Summit Drive.

Nichols's links to Grund were particularly close because the onetime prosecutor had saved his life during a scuba-diving accident in the Caribbean during which he suffered the bends. As tearaways in their late twenties and early thirties, Nichols and Grund would regularly double-date girls. They tended to go after sisters. The two men had seen each other virtually every day over the previous twenty years. They skied together, swam together, drank together, and played hard together.

But it must be remembered that Nichols's primary

reason for getting officially involved in the Grund murder case was his expertise at organizing covert police operations. He specialized in technical and drug investigations and was an expert phone surveillance—wiretapping—operative.

Nichols sometimes even carried out duties for the FBI and state-wide agencies. As such, he had become the self-proclaimed "Captain Gadget" of Miami County. There were also his other skills as a pilot which had unofficially come into use just twenty-four hours after Jimmy's murder and would no doubt be put to use again during the later stages of the investigation.

Nichols already had unofficially linked up with his old buddy and fellow Shanty Malone's regular Wil Siders a few days after Jim Grund had been buried. The two men already jointly had exerted some pressure on their chief suspect for his murder—Susan Grund. And now they were going to step up the psychological warfare.

They intended to pile the heat on Susan, since there was still absolutely no hard and fast evidence linking her to the murder.

The police plan that revolved around Florida businessman Jack Vetter was to lure Susan to a meeting with Vetter at the Signature Inn, near Peru. Two rooms were rented; one for Vetter and Susan and the other for officers to set up surveillance equipment. As the chief wire technician, Gary Nichols was on hand to monitor the entire operation.

Susan arrived at the Signature on the afternoon of August 20, 1992, at approximately 4:30 P.M. after agreeing to meet Vetter following a call made by him to her rented home in Vincennes. Susan was driving her sister Darlene's blue car. She met with Vetter in the room and they talked for three hours. The entire conversation was recorded, but Susan was incredibly careful not to say anything incriminating. Even when Vetter led Susan to believe that the police were closer to arresting her than they really were, she did not falter. At one stage, Vetter even offered to hide her murder weapon, but Susan coolly replied she had no knowledge of the handgun.

In the room next door, Gary Nichols and the Indiana state troopers were sweating profusely in the scorching heat. But throughout the three hours, Susan kept her head in a remarkably professional manner. The surveillance team were bitterly disappointed when she left the motel room at around 7:30 P.M. They had heard absolutely nothing that would help them prove that she had murdered her husband. In fact, it was plainly obvious that Susan had sussed out the sting the moment she met Vetter.

Investigators continued to keep an eye on Susan even after that failed operation. In some instances, they knew she knew she was being followed, but that was all part of the psychological warfare being waged against her by representatives of three different law enforcement agencies.

Gary Nichols and Jimmy Grund had been planning to buy a plane together shortly before he died to replace the one he had sold a couple of years previously because of the financial strain of keeping Susan in clothes and property. In Nichols's mind that was just another reason to track her down and bring her to justice.

On August 24, ISP Investigator Bob Brinson got word that Susan had enjoyed an illicit affair with a member of a local charity group, whom she had met through her work as an organizer for various local beauty pagcants.

Rumors had been circulating that Susan had been regularly seen out with the man and there were clear implications that sex was involved. When interviewed by investigators, the man admitted he knew Susan and had shared a few drinks with her at Shanty Malone's. The man even nervously confessed that he had told Susan his own marriage was in trouble. He insisted that Susan had given him some very good advice and that, as a result, he had repaired his own marriage. But he emphatically denied he had an affair with Susan. Now it seemed that besides being someone who adored sleeping with strange men, Susan was also a skilled marriage counselor. The investigators were bemused to say the least, but decided to give the man the benefit of the doubt. In any case, it was hardly as if he was the only man in Miami County to have slept with Susan Grund.

That same day, the state police unit served a subpoena on the Peru Trust Company located in Peru. The subpoena was to produce any records of an existing trust fund for Tanelle Rachelle Grund. It turned out that the trust for $25,000 had actually been established on July 19, 1985. With interest it had leapt up to $31,793.17 by the time the investigators got to it. It had not been touched by either Susan or her husband. Investigator Brinson was intrigued by the discovery of the trust because it totally contradicted what he was beginning to perceive as Susan's *modus operandi*. Obviously, when it came to her own flesh and blood she could be as loyal and as generous as any other parent.

# Fourteen

On August 27, the Indiana State Police unit talked to the father of a little boy who went to school with Tanelle Grund and had been with the Grunds on the day of July 4 when David's gun was allegedly stolen. It emerged that this father had been over to Susan's house to drop off his son who was going to let off some fireworks with Tanelle and a handful of neighborhood children in the backyard. At about 10:00 P.M. Susan dropped off the little boy at his father's house.

The man's testimony seemed to tally with what they already knew, but then the man pulled out his pocket computer calendar and consulted it carefully to reveal that on August 20—sixteen days after the killing of Jimmy Grund—Susan had called him because she wanted to borrow his pickup truck to move some belongings to Vincennes. According to the man, Susan then brought up the subject of David's gun being stolen and said that David was a suspect, but that she didn't think he would kill Jim. Susan even made a point of saying to the man that the gun had been stolen on the same night that the man's son had been round at the Grund house for the fireworks display. She also told him that the gun was probably the one used to kill her husband.

The man was astounded by the way the conversation was developing because she sounded more like a detective than a grieving widow. Then Susan rounded it off with an even more remarkable statement: "Jim took two files with him to Alaska for our vacation and I suspect that there was something in those files that got him killed."

It seemed as if she was deliberately planting information with the man in the hope he would tell the police what he knew.

Instead of thinning out like most investigations, this one was gaining even more twists and turns.

On August 29, 1992, there was another murder in the Peru area, one that would be completely overshadowed by the Grund investigation.

Toni A. Spicer, twenty-seven, was found strangled to death in her home at the Maple Lawn trailer park, just south of Indiana 18 highway. The young mother's body was discovered at 7:00 A.M. by a baby-sitter, who was bringing home the single mother's children.

Spicer had last been seen alive at the Hip Hugger, a dance bar and restaurant in Kokomo where she worked as a dancer. Her death could not have been more in contrast with the murder of Jim Grund. But Toni Spicer's lifestyle represented precisely the world that Susan had managed to escape from, although, ironically, that didn't stop Susan from being drawn into tragedy.

\*   \*   \*

As Bob Brinson's methodical investigation gained momentum, Gary Nichols, Wil Siders, and other investigators were continuing their occasional surveillance of Susan at her new base in Vincennes. Both men firmly believed that sooner or later Susan would make a mistake.

On August 31, 1992, Brinson and his unit of investigators flew to Oklahoma City with Wil Siders. The team was met at the airport by a member of the local FBI and the group headed to the County Prosecutor's Office to meet with Assistant D.A. Ray Elliott. Elliott provided the investigators with the criminal files on the child battery arrest and charges concerning Susan Whited, as she was then known. After reviewing the files, Bob Brinson traveled to the offices of attorney Bruce Winston, who represented Susan's third husband, Thomas Whited, Jr. Mr. Winston agreed to copy and mail portions of Susan Grund's testimony in reference to the civil suit filed against her by the paternal grandfather of tragic little Tommy.

The following day, Brinson and his colleagues flew on to Colorado Springs where they interviewed Gary Campbell at his place of employment, the Chapel Hills Mall. Once again, to keep to official protocol, the unit was escorted to the meeting with Campbell by a member of the local FBI.

For Brinson, the interview with Campbell proved a real eye-opener because it revealed more details about the "business transactions" concerning the custody of Jacob, including the wedding that was paid for by Jimmy Grund.

Campbell was able to prove to investigators that he was in Colorado Springs on the night of the murder of Jimmy Grund and when the gun was stolen a month earlier, he was at home watching a fireworks display.

On September 2, 1992, another of Susan's gentleman friends called in at Brinson's unit at the Indiana State Police Post in Peru to report that she had telephoned him from her mobile phone that very day to ask him to meet her for lunch in Indianapolis. Susan also asked if he would like to go to the Colts ball game that weekend, but her friend declined the invitation and they promised to speak again in the near future. Obviously, Susan Grund was not going to let the murder of her husband get in the way of her having a good time.

Brinson reckoned this call was very significant because it clearly showed that far from mourning her dearly departed husband, she was hungrily looking around for a man to seduce.

That same day, Jan Fern, wife of Jim Grund's law partner Don Fern called Bob Brinson's unit to report a significant conversation she had with Susan on July 12, three weeks before the murder.

Jan revealed that Susan had discussed working in the flower bed behind the house on Summit Drive and how she had gotten calluses on her hands. Jan had been astonished by this because Susan was not exactly known as a keen gardener. Susan also kept waffling on about redoing the back yard so it wouldn't look so messy.

The investigators were intrigued by Jan Fern's call because it seemed to suggest that Susan may have kept something carefully buried in the back yard between the time of the theft of David Grund's gun and the murder of Jimmy Grund.

The following day, a search warrant was served at the Grund residence giving the probable cause that Susan possibly had been digging and hiding the gun which was stolen from David Grund. It was all part of the pressure tactics Wil Siders had decided should be a crucial part of their effort to wear down Susan Grund until she made a mistake.

The search warrant team included Sgt. Dcan Marks of the ISP, who swept the ground outside the house on Summit Drive with a metal detector, along with Trooper Paul Daugherty, Sgt. Phil Oliver, Sgt. Bob Land, Sgt. Pat O'Connor, and Bob Brinson. The investigators entered the house by removing the garage door casing and inner garage door casing. But no items were found and nothing was seized.

Bob Brinson was naturally disappointed by his failure to find anything, but what he did not realize was that the raid on the house on Summit Drive was sending shock waves through Susan's immediate family.

To start with, Susan—living in Vincennes by now—panicked when she heard about the search and called her sister Darlene. Susan instructed Darlene to go out to the house to make sure it was secure.

After doing that, Darlene walked across the green that separated the house from other properties and called Susan again from a neighbor's house to say that everything looked in order.

"I want you to break back into the house and see if they found it," explained a breathless and clearly flustered Susan.

Darlene was astonished. She presumed "it" meant the gun. At first, she did not respond.

Susan continued, "I want you to go into the laundry room and then call me and tell me 'yes' or 'no.'"

"No way, Susan," came Darlene's reply. But Susan was being very forceful and she had always been the pushy one in the family, the leader of the pack.

A few minutes later, Darlene found a hammer in the neighbor's garage and went back to the house, intending to break a window. But her husband George turned up just before she was about to do it and talked her out of it.

Darlene called Susan back and told her, "If it's so important, why don't you come up here and do it yourself."

Susan was furious. She wanted to check the place out before the investigators had a chance to come back. But she could tell from the tone of her sister's voice that her scheme was not going to work.

Susan then came up with a plan to meet her sister in Indianapolis and then return with her to search the house. Darlene agreed and even managed to persuade neighbor Mary Pruitt to go along with her to offer moral support and provide a decoy car to put investigators off the scent.

At approximately 4:00 A.M. the three women met in the parking lot of a garage next to a McDonald's. Susan asked Mary to drive her vehicle, and Susan then got into Darlene's car with her and they returned to Peru together. Throughout the journey, Susan ducked down whenver she thought she saw any police cruisers.

As Darlene drove, her sister said to her, "I want you to promise me something."

Darlene reckoned she knew precisely what was coming.

"I don't make promises until I know what I'm promising."

"I have to tell you something and you can't tell a soul. . . . I shot Jimmy. It was supposed to be a murder/suicide."

According to Susan, Jim was despondent about getting old and fat and losing her to a younger man.

Susan said that Jim told her if he killed himself the insurance would not pay off to the children.

Susan also claimed that after killing Jim Grund, she didn't commit suicide because Grund only put one bullet in the gun and she didn't know how to reload it.

Leo Leger was asleep when he heard a loud knocking at the door of his house in the town of Kokomo, about two-thirds of the way from Indianapolis to Peru.

He got up and went to the door to see who on earth could be stopping by at this late hour. Standing there was his ex-girlfriend, Darlene Worden. The two sisters had stopped at Leo's home so that Darlene could use the bathroom.

She walked straight past him in a highly agitated state.

"Honey, you okay?" asked Leger.

"No," Darlene hesitated for a moment. Then she went on, "My sister wants to commit suicide because she killed her husband." If it hadn't been so tragic, it would have been funny. It actually sounded like the sort of thing Peg Bundy would say on Susan's favorite TV show, *Married . . . With Children.*

Leger—who did not know Susan well—had no idea who her husband was. But when it was explained to him that it was Jimmy Grund, he said, "Oh my goodness. Maybe we should bring her out from the car and talk to her."

Moments later, a very flustered Susan came in to Leo Leger's home. She pointed an accusing finger at Leger and screamed, "You told him, didn't you?"

Susan was furious with her sister and wanted to know exactly what Darlene had told him. Darlene then admitted she had told Leo about Susan wanting to commit suicide. Susan rolled her eyes to the ceiling and realized she had broken the golden rule—don't tell anyone what you have done. But there was no turning back now, so she told Darlene to hurry up, and a few minutes later they continued their journey to Peru.

Darlene deposited her sister at the end of the drive to the house at Summit and drove her car up alongside the garage doors. Darlene got out, unlocked the front door, and then Susan emerged from the shadows in the backyard and followed her inside the house. She had become so paranoid about the police that she did not want them to see her going into the house.

Darlene watched Susan go into the laundry room and emerge with two Christmas teddy bears, which she dropped into a black plastic trash bag. She did not dare ask what they were for. She had a pretty good idea, anyhow.

Then they left the house and drove directly to Darlene's home on East 3rd Street, in Peru. On the way, Susan turned to her sister and said, "I heard that metal detectors can't detect through cement."

Darlene knew exactly what her sister was talking about, but she chose to ignore it in the hope it would all go away.

At the house, Susan asked Darlene for some cotton so she could sew up the back of one of the teddy bears. Then she went down into the basement of the house and finished off her needlework.

When Susan came back upstairs she suggested to her sister that she should swap cars again because she suspected the police might follow her. So, Susan drove Darlene's husband's pickup truck back to her refuge in Vincennes clutching the teddy bear that hid the murder weapon. Once back at the house, Susan put the gun and the bear downstairs, away from the children.

The next day, Darlene had to drive back to Vincennes and switch vehicles.

Throughout all this, Nellie Sanders was getting very nervous at the house she was now sharing with Susan in Vincennes. She knew the gun was on the property and she advised her daughter to get rid of it as quickly as possible. That day, Nellie went to her nephew Donny's house and came back with a rusty old metal container. Susan then phoned Darlene in Peru and asked her to bring some concrete with her because she wanted to "bury it."

Next day, mother and daughter mixed the concrete and poured it slowly all over the gun as it lay in the base of that metal container. Then they let it set for a couple of days.

A few days later they poured some earth over the top of the hardened concrete and put a plant in the container. It seemed like the perfect hiding place.

Some weeks later, Nellie Sanders got very twitchy about having the container in the house in Vincennes and insisted it had to go. Eventually, she put it in Susan's van and the two women hauled it round to nephew Donny Ellis's house, where Nellie somehow managed to single-handedly carry the seventy-three-pound container upstairs and dump it in the attic.

After a few days, Susan's son Jacob asked his mother once again about the inserts he had read in her diary the previous spring. The references to divorce and marriage problems had taken on much more significance since the death of Jimmy Grund. Susan looked at Jacob distastefully and acted as if she didn't know anything about any diary. Jacob did not pursue the matter, but he had a pretty good idea of what was going on.

Back at the Miami County courthouse office of Jim Grund's old friend county prosecutor Wil Siders, efforts to gather enough evidence to arrest Susan were still failing to provide anything truly conclusive, although Siders was still as convinced as ever that she was the killer.

State police investigators and all other officials involved in the case met with Siders on September 17 to discuss the inquiry and hold a brainstorming session to try and come up with some fresh leads.

In the *Peru Daily Tribune,* Indiana State Police Lt. Carlos Pettiford said he believed the case would eventually be solved and he talked about "strong leads." But nobody yet had enough to even consider convicting Susan Grund and as long as that situation continued there was no question of arresting her for the murder of her husband.

At the Indiana State Police Post, the four weeks between mid-September and mid-October were pretty quiet for the investigation. Bob Brinson had tried everything to subtly put pressure on Susan, but she had survived intact. He remained fairly convinced about her guilt, but he started to wonder if any weak areas would ever begin to emerge.

On September 30, another member of Peru's elite upper middle class came forward to state that Susan had told her that she and Jim were having marital problems just a few weeks before his death. The most interesting aspect of this woman's claims was that she said that Susan had told her that "the things that brought them together were now the things that were problems." Those two things were:

1. Initially, Jim had liked Susan to dress sexy and now he was upset when she did.
2. At the beginning of the marriage, Jim had been strong and taken charge. Now Susan wasn't getting that leadership from him.

Susan's frank statement to her friend astonished Bob Brinson. Here was a strong-willed, powerful lady apparently complaining because her husband was not bossy enough! Susan Grund was emerging as an increasingly complex character.

The same informant also told Brinson that Susan had regularly discussed Jim's will in the preceding few years and was concerned about her husband's law firm partner Don Fern having too much power as administrator of the will.

On October 1, 1992, Brinson and his unit managed to trace one of the businessmen rumored to be having an affair with Susan. He told investigators that he was part of the lunch group which met on Wednesdays and stated that they consisted of a local attorney, an insurance salesman, an accountant and an attorney, plus himself. The meals were usually held at the local Holiday Inn.

The man emphatically denied ever having a physical relationship with Susan Grund. He admitted attending a fund-raising event in Peru when both Susan and Jim were present. The man even attended the funeral of Jim Grund, but insisted he had not seen Susan since that sad occasion. He also conceded that she had called him on September 29 and given him her unlisted phone number at her mother's home near Vincennes. "She told me not to let anyone have it," he explained.

\*   \*   \*

During the week of October 8, 1992, Brinson finally received a copy of the toxicology report prepared by the Indiana University School of Medicine. The report was prepared from blood and urine specimens collected by technicians from the body of James Grund. But no drugs were found, and he had an alcohol level of just .05 percent.

In early October, a state police diving team drew a complete blank when they searched for the weapon used in Jimmy's murder. Nine divers examined a stretch of the river that runs through the center of Peru for five hours. To onlookers, it appeared as if investigators had been told where to find the gun, but—it later emerged—the divers were on a speculative venture hastened by the investigators' desperation for some positive proof to link the murder to Susan Grund.

The police divers scoured the areas near the town's two main bridges in the hope of finding the gun. But they never came close to discovering anything.

On October 9, Susan's role as the main suspect in the murder of her husband was made public thanks to a civil suit which alleged she was under investigation for the homicide. The suit was brought by David Grund and his sister Jama Anne Lidral to try and prevent Susan from being an executor of Jimmy Grund's will. They clearly stated that the will filed on September 11 was not intended to be their father's last will. David and Jama insisted that the only valid will was one dated October 31, 1986.

Documents filed October 9 described the July 17 will as "a fraud" and reiterated that the will was obtained under coercion.

The legal complaint to resist probate of Jimmy Grund's will was filed at the Miami County courthouse. The request asked for a jury and petitioned for appointment of a special administrator. In short, Jim Grund's two eldest children were challenging the legality of the will made by their father just before his death.

The complaint clearly stated that:

1. Grund had died leaving two wills.
2. The deceased was survived by the plaintiffs, David Grund and Jama Lidral, and by the defendant, Susan A. Grund and her two (2) children, Jacob James Grund and Tanelle Rachelle Grund, who were only his heirs-at-law.

The complaint also revealed that Jimmy Grund owed more than $173,000 in mortgage and loan repayments at the time of his death and that was costing the estate $42.88 a day in interest.

Susan's civil case attorney, Stephen Blower, filed a change of venue with the court and a hearing was arranged for October 19. A special administrator was appointed to handle the estate while the complaint was being tried.

In contesting the will, Jimmy Grund's two eldest children were claiming that Susan was not qualified to be an executor to the estate and was not entitled to be sole beneficiary of their father's estate. State law did not allow a person to be an executor if there was a felony conviction.

The filing of the suit had the side effect of unofficially informing the entire community that Susan was officially suspected to be the killer of her husband. Now she had no hiding place, even though she was still at liberty.

And on October 12, prosecutor Wil Siders decided

to pile even further pressure on Susan by giving an interview to the *Peru Daily Tribune*.

Headlined, SIDERS: SUSAN GRUND A SUSPECT, the article began, "The wife of James H. Grund is a suspect in his slaying, Prosecutor Wil Siders confirmed Monday. . . ."

But the most significant part of the article referred to November 14, 1983, when Susan, then known as Susan Whited, pleaded guilty to misdemeanor child beating. That meant she was automatically disqualified from being an executor on Jimmy's will, according to state laws.

The *Tribune* even tracked down Oklahoma City Assistant D.A. Don Deason, who confirmed to the newspaper that a plea agreement was entered by Susan after her former husband, Tom Whited, had reconciled with her.

Siders decided to make the double bombshell announcement to the newspaper in the light of the civil complaint filed by David and Jama. It was clearly a carefully considered decision deliberately intended to make Susan feel even less secure. The knives were out for her. There was no point in pretending anymore—as far as Wil Siders and the entire Grund family were concerned, Susan murdered Jimmy and she was already a convicted child batterer.

On October 19, Bob Brinson and his team of investigators received evidence that Susan—who claimed to have lost a lot of jewelry in the so-called burglary that resulted in her husband's death—was rarely seen wearing any expensive jewelry. This clearly implied she did not own the quantity of gems she had earlier claimed.

Jim Grund's sister Jane and her husband Fred,

Jim's partner in the car dealership, insisted to investigators they had never seen Susan with expensive jewelry. Susan wore costume jewelry most of the time and Jane could only recall Jim Grund buying his wife one expensive gold ring.

On November 1, 1992, a very strange incident occurred. It was something that has never been satisfactorily explained.

Bob Brinson was contacted by David Grund who wanted him to know that he suspected someone had tried to break into his home on East Main Street that very day, while he was out. Brinson immediately went to the apartment to investigate. It appeared that David Grund was moving into another residence and thought someone had disturbed his gun cleaning kit. Nothing else was reported disturbed.

While Brinson was still at David's apartment, his mother Jane arrived on the scene. She was very concerned about her son's safety and she agreed to an interview with Bob Brinson, who had not spoken to her during the earlier part of his investigation.

The pieces to the jigsaw were getting bigger but there was no obvious solution in sight.

# Fifteen

The first days of November gave warning that the chilling discomfort of winter would soon arrive in northern Indiana. The blustery winds that swept across Miami County took on a hard bite that sent dairy farmers in search of heavy jackets and wives to the closets for additional quilts for the bed. Outside chores were accomplished with a quicker step, the reward for their hurried completion being a return to the warmth indoors.

Men lingered longer over coffee in Peru's main coffeeshops, and women quick-stepped from their cars into the grocery store or post office, no longer stopping to chat in the parking lot. To the casual observer, it appeared the people of Peru had fallen back into a normal routine. Below the surface, however, a pervasive feeling of despondency shrouded the town.

Over evening meals, residents talked about their suspicions concerning the main suspect in the killing of Jimmy Grund—his wife Susan. At work, people tried at first to discourage speculation about the murder, then it became clear that discussion of the tragedy was the prime subject on everyone's mind.

The month had come with a great rush. On the international scene, the fighting in Croatia continued unabated and with the presidential election just days away, George Bush tried hard to paint his democratic challenger Bill Clinton as deceitful and deceptive. But most polled expressed disbelief over Bush's explanation of his involvement in the Iran-Contra scandal.

Interesting stuff, but in Peru there was only one story, and it appeared to be going nowhere fast until—on November 2, 1992—an increasingly nervous Darlene Worden, Susan's only sister in Peru, found herself lining up for her unemployment check at the Miami County courthouse in the center of town. Darlene had an extremely guilty conscience. As far as sisters went, Darlene and Susan had their problems, but she had always remained close to Susan. Darlene had been brought up by their mother Nellie to take care of her younger brothers and sisters and she felt a protective instinct when it came to Susan. She kept wondering what her father would have done if he had found himself in her situation.

Darlene had listened intently when Susan confessed to her about Jimmy's killing. She knew that Susan had only told her everything because she trusted her and looked up to her for advice. But Darlene was deeply troubled by what Susan had admitted. It wasn't right to murder anyone, let alone your own husband.

As Darlene walked out of the impressive grey stone courthouse building that morning she saw Indiana State Police Investigator Bob Brinson emerge from the sheriff's office just across from the back entrance to the courthouse. Darlene decided to approach Brinson because she needed to find out exactly what he knew about Susan's involvement.

Darlene might share the same deep, saucerlike brown eyes and and fresh honeydewed complexion as her sister, but there the similarities stop. Darlene is as shy as Susan is forward. And seeing Brinson—renowned locally as a solid, impartial law officer—made her feel very nervous because it reminded her of the whole dreadful situation.

She crossed the street and walked up to Brinson just as he was getting into his Ford Taurus. The investigator looked up the moment he saw Darlene and instinctively knew immediately that this could be the biggest breakthrough in the case. He got out of his car and they started talking. Then he offered Darlene a cup of coffee and a cookie in the privacy of the Miami County Sheriff's Department just across the street.

Darlene was shaking with nervousness. She didn't care about implicating herself. She was just very concerned about making sure her mother was not held responsible in any way. Darlene had made up her mind; her mother's liberty was more important than Susan's. That was the driving force behind her decision that morning.

Just a few hours later, Brinson had concluded that Darlene Worden's evidence was so vital to the case that he should hold an emergency meeting with Miami County Prosecutor Wil Siders. At that gathering in the attorney's courthouse offices, it was decided an attempt would be made to get Darlene and Susan together and record any conversation or admission by Susan Grund.

This time, the wiring *had* to work. The Grund case investigators fully realized that this was probably going to be their final chance to nail Susan for the murder of her husband.

Darlene was reluctant at first. The investigators insisted it was a life or death situation because they were convinced that Susan intended to harm her sister because she knew about Susan's involvement. Darlene was not so sure and wondered if these dramatic conclusions were just a ruse to ensure she went ahead with a sting operation on her sister.

But Wil Siders was most insistent and in the end, Darlene simply shrugged her shoulders and reluctantly agreed to help bring Susan to justice.

Stage one of the operation meant that Darlene had to immediately call up Susan and say she was going to bring some social security checks over to Vincennes for her, plus her mail from the house on Summit Drive.

When a very nervous Darlene made the call later that day, Susan was very suspicious.

"Why are you coming?" she asked her sister.

"I need to talk to you," replied Darlene.

After a bit more coaxing, Susan agreed and Darlene said she would see her in "a few hours."

Darlene was then wired up carefully by Gary Nichols so that he would be able to record the sound of a pin dropping from the moment his transmitter was turned on.

The five-hour drive to Vincennes was agonizing for Darlene. She could not make up her mind if she was doing the right thing. She hoped and prayed that Susan would not suspect anything. But Darlene felt edgy and she knew her sister well enough to realize that if she was even vaguely suspicious then she would never utter a word in relation to the case. Darlene also felt very torn because this was a blatant setup and her sister might well end up in jail as a result of her actions. Whatever she may or may not have done, it was not particularly pleasant to contemplate causing the imprisonment of your own sister.

Darlene was practically shaking by the time she got to the house in Vincennes. She felt more guilty than if she had committed the murder herself.

Sgt. Pat O'Connor, Trooper Gary Boyles, Sheriff Jack Rich, and Wil Siders, plus Bob Brinson, had followed her to Vincennes, hoping and praying that this might be the break they needed so desperately. All the investigators were extremely concerned about Darlene's highly emotional state, although they had no choice but to continue with the operation. This was their biggest chance so far to get enough evidence to arrest Susan Grund.

As she arrived at the house in her car, Darlene seriously contemplated abandoning the entire scheme. She would throw the transmitter down the toilet the moment she got inside the house, she decided.

At the door to greet her was her mother Nellie and nephew Jacob. They seemed so pleased to see her that it simply accentuated the pain and anguish Darlene was suffering. But something drove her on. Whether it was her own strongly held belief in right and wrong, or simply a fear that she might be implicated in helping her sister if she did not bring her to justice, no one will ever know.

But within a few minutes of arriving, Darlene and Susan were walking outside and talking. However, it wasn't going to be easy. Susan initially refused even to refer back to that trip to the house to take out the gun a few weeks earlier. She seemed incredibly wary of

Darlene. It was as if she had instantly worked out that her sister was wired.

Darlene became so tense it was obvious to Susan that something was seriously wrong and after a few minutes, she stopped and scribbled out a note to her sister asking her if she was wired.

In her appalling state of nervousness, Darlene was confused by the note at first, then she just ignored it. Susan, afraid to say anything in case it was heard by investigators, just continued walking.

All the time, the investigators' orders were ringing in Darlene's mind, so she still did as instructed and continued to try and pull the conversation round to whether her sister had killed Jim Grund.

"I know you can't remember what happened that evening, but you confessed to me you killed Jim," muttered a very nervous Darlene to her sister. It was pretty clumsy stuff.

"My God, Darlene, I never said anything like that to you at all. I don't understand why you are saying that."

Darlene was even more thrown by her sister's response, but she pressed on desperately, repeating the same thing over and over. In their listening post across the fields, the investigators were grimacing with embarrassment. This was looking like a complete disaster.

Eventually, Darlene and Susan returned to the house. Susan was furious, but she had kept her calm because she did not want anything incriminating to be recorded. Shortly afterwards, Darlene departed, having failed to get even remotely enough evidence.

The investigators sitting in their vehicles half a mile away were bitterly disappointed. It seemed as if Susan had once again managed to slip from their grasp. For a housewife with no previous criminal activities other than that child battery case in Oklahoma, she was proving a very slippery customer.

The operation had been a disaster. Bob Brinson really began to wonder if perhaps they had all under-estimated the intelligence of Susan Grund.

A few minutes later, Darlene met up with investigators and was told that they were going to go ahead and arrest Susan on the basis of what Darlene had told them in her statement about how the two sisters went back to the house to take the gun and the teddy bears. Darlene pleaded with them not to arrest Susan until the next morning for the sake of the children and her mother, Nellie. She thought an early morning raid would be very traumatic for the rest of the family.

But within the hour, Wil Siders and Bob Brinson met with Knox County Prosecutor Dale Webster at his office, near Vincennes. The unit signed a search warrant affidavit and the search warrant was signed and ordered by Knox County Superior Court Judge Edward Theobold. The unit returned to the Susan Grund residence located at 406 Locust Street and served the search warrant at 4:40 A.M. next morning.

No gun was located at the house, but the two Christmas teddy bears were found and seized. They clearly had been used to transport something of approximately the same size as the gun for which they were looking.

Bob Brinson arrested Susan Grund for the murder of James Grund as she stood and watched while investigators thoroughly searched the premises. She was immediately transported to Knox County Jail to be incarcerated for the remainder of that night. It was hoped that once all the correct paperwork had been completed she could be on her way back to Miami County.

Later that day, the *Peru Daily Tribune* screamed out the news that everyone had been expecting for weeks in a front-page headline: SUSAN GRUND FACES MURDER CHARGE.

The article began, "Susan Grund was jailed early today in Vincennes on a charge of murder for the death of her husband, James H. Grund.

"The arrest was made by Indiana State Police Senior Trooper Investigator Bob Brinson at 4:40 A.M. Susan, 34, was arrested at 406 Locust St., according to jailer John McKinnon at the Knox County Sheriff's Department."

No bond was set by the Knox County authorities, who expected Susan to be transported to the Miami County Jail in Peru within hours.

Reporters remember that day well because it just so happened to be the day that Bill Clinton won the battle for the White House in the presidential elections.

Prosecutor Wil Siders saw that date as being doubly significant. Election day may have brought the nation together, but the early morning arrest of Susan Grund that same day definitely brought a community together.

Other pressure was mounting on Susan thanks to further moves by her stepson and stepdaughter to prevent her from getting access to their father's will. First it was announced that Marvin D. McLaughlin, a retired judge from Starke Count Circuit Court, had been selected to preside over the hearings in the matter of the Grund estate.

Miami Circuit Judge Bruce Embrey even granted a change of venue of judge, and gave a panel of judges for attorneys Pat Roberts and Stephen Bower from which to choose. The fact Embrey was a close personal friend of Jimmy Grund and one of the first people at the murder scene following Susan's 911 call was never mentioned.

A few hours after Susan's arrest, Investigator Bob Brinson met with principal Paul Couchenour at the Clark Middle School in Vincennes. After advising Couchenour that he wanted to interview Jacob Grund, the principal provided a private office for the purpose. Sheriff Jack Rich was also present. Jacob was then informed that his mother was under arrest and he was asked if he had any information about the murder of his stepfather. Young Jacob was stunned and had no new information to tell the officers.

Also on November 3—at around 1:00 P.M.—Brinson's unit picked Susan Grund up from the Knox County Jail and and transported her back to Miami County Jail in Peru, where she was photographed and fingerprinted by Trooper Gary Boyles the following morning.

Meanwhile, Brinson's unit transported those two Christmas teddy bears back to the Indiana State Police Post in Peru. Trooper Dean Marks was instructed to have the bears examined for gunshot residue.

At last, the chief suspect in the murder of Jimmy Grund was behind bars. But there was still a long way to go before those charges could be made to stick.

# Sixteen

Miami County Prosecutor Wil Siders stood at the window of his small office, looking out into the greying twilight at the crowd that had gathered opposite at the jailhouse following Susan Grund's arrest. He counted half a dozen television minicams bearing the logos of stations from Indianapolis to Chicago. Reporters and photographers elbowing for space among a number of curious local citizens, encircled every cop—however junior—who emerged from the building.

Wil Siders then took a gulp of his lukewarm coffee and headed off for the assembled crowd. His body ached with fatigue following the activities of the previous twenty-four hours. But there was still one more important duty before he started assembling the case against Susan Grund.

Five minutes later, he stood on the steps outside the courthouse insisting that Susan had murdered her husband because she stood to inherit more than $200,000 from Jimmy Grund's will. Meanwhile, other stories circulating the town talked of her numerous illicit lovers.

Siders admitted to reporters, "There has been a tremendous amount of pressure on the community as a result of this crime." He also reiterated that there were no other suspects in the case, despite the other polygraph examinations carried out in the first few weeks of the investigation.

Siders also disclosed the help given to him by Susan's sister Darlene, even pausing to sympathize with the reasons why it took her so long to come forward.

"I can't fault anyone for not wanting to talk about their own flesh and blood, but there comes a point when conscience overcomes flesh and blood," he told reporters.

In Peru itself, there was much celebrating at the news of Susan's arrest. After all, she long had been considered by most of the town to be an evil woman. She'd been figuratively hung, drawn, and quartered long before her detainment in the early hours of the morning in Vincennes.

On November 4, Susan was escorted across the street from the Miami County Jail to the county courthouse for an initial hearing.

The courthouse, on the corner of Broadway and Main, is a building steeped in history, much of it linked to the man she was accused of murdering. Built in 1910 for the then not inconsiderable sum of $237,000, it cuts an impressive sight with its granite and limestone facade built in the classical revival style, with a dominant full-height porch and classical columns supporting the roof. Inside of the rotunda hung a fourteen foot replica of the U.S. Constitution signed by four thousand people in the town's bicentennial year of 1986.

In the courtroom, Judge Bruce Embrey read Susan her rights and told her that the penalties for murder, a class-A felony, were thirty to sixty years in prison. A not guilty plea was entered and Susan informed the judge, who she had last seen when he appeared at her house on the night of the shooting, that attorney Nick Thiros from Merrillville would represent her.

Embrey—well aware of his own personal interest in the case—immediately excused himself and offered the attorneys a panel of judges from which to choose.

The court heard that a probable cause affidavit had been filed by prosecutors that morning and it clearly stated that Susan knew her stepson had a gun because David's gun permit had been mailed to his father's house.

Afterwards, prosecutor Wil Siders made a plea to the public through the pages of the *Peru Daily Tribune*. "If there is anyone in the community that has evidence that might be relevant to this case, I welcome them to contact me, the state police, or sheriff's department."

Next day, November 4, the *Peru Daily Tribune* followed up its scoop on the arrest of Susan Grund with an article that featured a photograph of Susan in a designer power suit, a well-coiffured hairstyle, and clutching a Bible in her hand as she arrived at the Miami County Jail following her dramatic arrest in Vincennes.

At least she was still getting her picture in the newspaper.

Inside the jailhouse, Sheriff Jack Rich and his wife Linda made every effort to ensure that Susan felt at home. They rapidly found her to be very different from their usual customers.

Susan quickly took over the small lady's quarters in the jailhouse and began running beauty classes and hairdressing sessions for her fellow inmates.

Inside jail, Susan mothered the other women. She was a queen bee in many ways, always prepared to offer a shoulder to cry on for any unhappy inmates. She also had the unnerving knack of doing her hair in a different style virtually every day of the week.

Visitors to Susan inside the Miami County Jail were astonished at how easily she adjusted to prison life. She seemed to handle it like an overnight stay at a friend's house. In a way, she was right because most of the jail officials were at one time or another friends of her's and her husband's.

Sheriff Rich and his wife, Linda, who worked as matron to the women inmates, were incredibly proud of their jailhouse. "You won't find a jail in the whole of Indiana that is cleaner or a kitchen that serves such fine food. We treat people humanely here," boasted Sheriff Rich.

Susan was expected to wear regulation orange jumpsuits inside the jail and her main visitor throughout her incarceration in Peru was one-time attorney and close friend John O'Neill, who lived in nearby Logansport. He knew both Jim and Susan through his family cabin which was near the Grund cabin on Max inkuckee Lake. He was the man with whom Susan had first struck up a friendship just a few months after her marriage to Jim Grund.

O'Neill became such a regular visitor that jail staff soon started calling him by his first name. He was seen holding Susan's hand as they talked in the visitor's room.

Inside the county jail, Susan continued to be immaculately turned out. She even had her own curling

iron and a vanity case loaded with beautician items.
She did it all herself and was always happy to help the
other women inmates glam up themselves a bit.

After a few months of wearing the jail's orange regulation jumpsuit, Susan was allowed to wear her own
clothes, although life inside the jail remained very
regimented in most other ways.

All inmates were woken up at 6:30 A.M. and expected to get their breakfast from the kitchen by 7:00
A.M. This consisted of cereal, fruit, coffee, and orange
juice. Hot oatmeal was provided three times a week.
That was followed by Bible studying.

At one stage, Susan had so many priests visiting her
that Sheriff Jack Rich insisted she decide which one
should take priority. He quietly explained that while
the jail might be obligated to allow men of God to see
their inmates, six ministers every week lining up to see
the beautiful alleged murderess was rather excessive.
He threatened to stop all her visitation rights unless
she cut down on these so-called spiritual advisors. She
stuck to one minister from then on.

Lunch inside the Miami County Jail was served at
11:15 A.M. It consisted of things like barbecue sand-
wiches and sour cream wedges. Susan and all the
other inmates had to pay for their own coffee or so-
das.

In the evening, dinner was served beginning at 4:30
P.M. Chicken patties, beans, and mashed potatoes
were a favorite. Once a week, desserts were provided
by jailhouse cook Sue Hall and once a month she
would bake a special cake for all the inmates.

By all accounts, Susan Grund rarely finished her
meal, preferring to keep an eye on her svelte figure
which she also kept in shape by taking as much regular exercise as possible.

In the evening, between 7:00 P.M. and 10:00 P.M., there was exercise on the roof terrace or at the gym in the basement, depending on the weather and time of year. Table tennis, basketball, and weight machines were also available.

At one point during Susan's stay in the county jail, the women's section became unusually crowded with inmates. They were a varied bunch, including a woman accused of trying to hire a hitman to kill her husband, and drug and alcohol offenders. Not surprisingly, Susan and the murder-for-hire lady found they had a lot in common. The woman was eventually released and the charges dropped against her when her husband decided he did not want to give evidence against her and they got back together.

A telephone in the cell could be used at any time, but was only available for collect calls. A TV set behind a glass screen provided the entertainment. The clicker was often the subject of heated discussions about which program to watch.

The forty or so men held in the male section immediately next door were supposed to never actually be seen by the female inmates. But, inevitably, love notes and trysts occasionally ocurred and Susan was not above a little harmless flirtation with some of the male trustees at meal times.

A bathroom off the main cell area provided the only privacy in the entire building. Susan sometimes spent ages locked in there with her thoughts, considering her next move.

Susan played at being the upper-class lady inside the Miami County Jail, but then, compared with most of the other inmates, she was well qualified. Sometimes she seemed a little aloof as she spent hours each day pouring over her dozens of religious books.

Susan developed quite a penchant for cook Sue Hall's special-recipe fruit sticks. But she had the annoying habit of clicking her well-manicured fingernails on the stainless steel counter at the canteen while waiting to be served her food at mealtime. She would then look up and give the male trustees a sickly sweet smile.

During her frequent court appearances, Susan put on a mask of seriousness and respectability the moment she caught sight of the press swarming around her as she exited the jailhouse before making the twenty-yard walk across this street to the courthouse. The only time that mask would drop in public was when she spotted a friend in the public gallery. Then a brief smile would come to her lips.

Susan got a visit from her sister Darlene soon after her arrest. It was a frosty encounter, by all accounts.

Susan immediately asked her sister why she had told the police the story about her confessing to Jimmy's murder as they drove up from that rendezvous near Indianapolis to the Summit Drive house in the early hours of the morning a few weeks after the killing.

Susan insisted to her sister that Darlene was either being paid by investigators, or someone was threatening her in order to get her to tell the story.

"I just had to tell it. I can't explain why," replied a very nervous Darlene.

The two sisters did manage a few more words including an extraordinarily insensitive request from Darlene to buy her sister's camper. Susan did not think that was a very good idea under the circumstances.

Then Susan scribbled a note on a scrap of paper and shoved it in front of her sister. It read, "They were in the woods waiting for me." She also referred to people who were planning to go into the jail to kill her because she knew the "true story."

Susan insisted that people like Judge Bruce Embrey and other old friends of her husband were out to get revenge and frame her for the murder of her husband.

A few days later, Susan called her sister collect on the Miami County Jail phone and told her to change her story. Darlene was outraged. "You take a polygraph and I'll talk."

"I said, change your story." There was an unpleasant tone to Susan's voice.

Then Darlene became very angry with her sister. She called her some nasty names and slammed the phone down. They have not talked to each other since.

Susan's arrest also sparked a storm of interest from the media outside Peru. The case was soon featured on nationwide TV news and the tabloid shows. Reporters from programs such as *Hard Copy, Inside Edition,* and *A Current Affair* started invading the town.

But Peru was not going to be intimidated. Most of the people approached for interviews turned down all journalists point-blank and one reporter from *Hard Copy* complained, "I can't find people who are willing to talk about it. It's as if the whole town has shut us out."

Even attorneys approached by the tabloid shows were reluctant to get drawn into a discussion about the case, let alone allow cameras into their offices and homes. It seemed as if Peru's ruling class was managing to stifle any interest from outsiders. The attitude seemed to be, *This is our problem and we will deal with it in our own way.*

Investigators were under heavy pressure from Miami County Prosecutor Wil Siders and others not to discuss the case publicly because they did not want to give away anything to the defense camp. But there may have also been a hidden agenda; aspects of the case such as David's alleged affair with Susan were not deemed fit for public consumption. The Grund family refused to accept that there could be a grain of truth in the rumors and they wanted to make sure they were not repeated—anywhere.

Meanwhile, David Grund went off to law school and was conspicuous by his absence from Peru. He would not talk to anyone about the case, least of all any of the pushy tabloid reporters in town.

On November 20, Susan decided to take advantage of her right to strike certain judges from the list of potential law officers to preside over her eventual trial by filing a motion through her then lawyer Nick Thiros to have Judge Edward J. Meyers removed from the list. It was never disclosed what Susan had against Judge Meyers.

One of Susan's oldest friends, Mary Heltzel, received a letter from Susan in January 1993.

The letter was identifiable because the words, THIS STAMP IDENTIFIES THIS CORRESPONDENCE AS HAVING BEEN MAILED BY AN OFFENDER INCARCERATED IN THE MIAMI COUNTY DETENTION CENTER, were emblazoned across the back of the envelope.

In the letter, postmarked January 26, 1993, Susan coolly acknowledged a card Mary had sent to her at the county jail. Then she went on to talk about her ailments, a fall inside the jail, a so-called blood clot, and she also claimed she had hurt her hip and her knee in another accident. None of these injuries turned out to be as serious as she had implied.

Susan's weight had plummetted to under ninety pounds and she insisted she was going to pray for "a speedy end to this nightmare."

But she then referred in a remarkably offhand way to the fate of her two children, Jacob and Tanelle. "The kids are with Mother," she wrote, "and doing as well as can be expected having lost essentially both of their parents." That was it, no guilt or sorrow just the distinct impression that the whole world was against her.

In religious matters, Susan was growing increasingly obsessed with the church. "God took Jim for a reason and he will continue to care for me and my children and will end this injustice soon," she ended her letter to Mary, which was signed "Prayfully your friend, Susan."

Also in January 1993, a tentative date had been set to begin Susan's murder trial. Special Judge John F. Surbeck, Jr., of Allen County Superior Court, had been chosen to preside over the hearing and he estimated it would last no more than one week once jury selection had been completed.

Susan appeared in the Miami County courthouse that day alongside a new attorney, Charlie Scruggs. Scruggs entered a plea of not guilty on behalf of Susan after it was revealed that her original attorney Nick J. Thiros had filed a motion to withdraw from the case for reasons unknown.

Charlie Scruggs, based in nearby Kokomo, was a scrupulously fair-minded attorney with experience on both sides of the legal barrier. He was no bright-eyed idealist searching for a cause. Neither was he an ambitious young defense lawyer seeking a high-profile client in hopes that the publicity would propel him on the path to money and celebrity. Scruggs was a shrewd, experienced, somewhat droll lawyer who looked like a smartly-dressed farmer and sounded like Gary Cooper.

In his office, a plaque on the wall proudly stated his motto as being, *When you've got them by the balls their hearts and minds will follow.*

Scruggs was a self-confessed race-car nut originally from Indianapolis. An attorney for thirty years, he had served six years at the nearby Marin County Prosecutor's Office before a ten-year stint at the U.S. Attorney's Office in Indianapolis.

But life back in Indianapolis turned sour when his wife announced she was leaving him. As Charlie Scruggs says now with a wry smile on his face, "The law is a jealous mistress. If you do it seriously you can have no other life."

But Scruggs still did have his beloved Harley motorcycle. On quiet days he brought it to the office and tinkered about with it in the parking lot. He called those sessions "making love."

In the corner of Scruggs's office is a cabinet filled with guns from the murder cases he has won over the years. He takes them off acquitted clients as a momento after proclaiming to them, "You can't handle it, so I'm taking it."

The one thing Charlie Scruggs will not talk about is the bombing outside a court a few years back that left him with a severe limp and ruined his chances of continuing his other love, skiing.

Charlie's take on Susan was blunt and to the point: "She's the kind of woman who in the proper atmosphere could cause a man's heart to beat faster than a Chevy push rod."

Charlie Scruggs spent hours examining all the evidence and newspaper clippings on the case when he was approached to become Susan's attorney. Following a three-hour meeting with her inside the Miami County jailhouse, he came away convinced of her innocence.

Scruggs knew full well that Susan was not liked in the community, but he believed that was mainly because she was a very beautiful woman who was "kinda racy." In a small town like Peru, women like Susan Grund needed to walk very softly or they'd soon find the whole place against them. Scruggs believed a lot of people had condemned Susan too hurriedly. There were also definite aspects of the case that left the whole investigation wide open.

To start with, *everyone* just assumed Susan was guilty. Scruggs did not see it that way and that was why he took the case. He was also impressed by Susan's articulate mannerisms. She was, in his opinion, a very believable person.

However, from inside her cell at the Miami County Jail, it would have been difficult for Susan Grund not to be left with the distinct impression that the entire town of Peru was after her blood.

At the beginning of December, all Jimmy Grund's real estate was placed on the open market for public sale. Special Judge Marvin D. McLaughlin ordered the sale after close consultation with attorneys Pat Roberts, Stephen Blower, Tom Keith, and specially appointed administrator Phil Tomson.

It was agreed that funds from the sale would be held in escrow by Tomson until further instructions were ordered by the court. McLaughlin also ordered an immediate inventory of all personal property within the house on Summit Drive. A hearing was set for February 12, 1993, to determine what would happen to Susan's half of the assets of the property, because of special state rules that insisted a person could not profit from murder if convicted.

To add to the confusion of the situation for the two most innocent members of the entire case—Susan's children, Tanelle and Jacob—it was decided that attorneys had to be appointed to represent their interests.

In Oklahoma City, Assistant D.A. Don Deason got a phone call from a reporter on the *Peru Daily Tribune* asking him about Susan's background. He had already heard through the grapevine that years earlier she had married an attorney and moved back to Indiana. He had always wondered who the lawyer was and whether he knew what he was getting into with a lady like Susan.

Now he had the ultimate evidence. It made him even more relieved he hadn't accepted her offer of a drink following that child battery case.

During a pretrial hearing on January 13, 1993, to discuss defense objections to holding the trial in Miami County, Susan appeared in court dressed in a long, woollen red coat over orange prison pants and white tennis shoes and socks. She closely studied a yellow legal pad before her attorney Charlie Scruggs arrived and the hearing began.

Susan's wavy blond hair neatly framed her lightly made-up face. A gold and gemstone ring glittered from the wedding finger of her left hand. She never took off her coat throughout the hearing.

Charlie Scruggs told the court there were numerous reasons why it would be deeply prejudicial for his client's murder trial to be heard in Miami County. They were:

1. Earlier public hostility against the defendant.
2. Public outrage over the offense.
3. Prejudicial news reporting or editorializing, which castigated the defendant.
4. Speculative opinions as to the personality and character of the accused.
5. Disclosures of inadmissible evidence.
6. Prior criminal records.

Scruggs even handed out copies of news articles written on the case that had appeared in the *Peru Daily Tribune.* Scruggs was clearly convinced that Susan would not receive a fair trial.

In March 1993, it was announced that initial objections to Susan Grund's trial being held in Miami County had been overruled, just so long as the eventual jury selected would be from nearby Kosciusko County. Special Judge John F. Surbeck reiterated that he expected the trial to last no more than two weeks. A final pretrial conference was scheduled for May 2 at 1:00 P.M.

Also in March, Susan found herself starring in the local newspapers yet again as arguments were heard in Miami County Circuit Court to determine if she was entitled to at least one-half of the sale of the Jimmy Grund's real estate proceeds, or if the money should be held in a trust pending the outcome of her criminal charge.

"She cannot profit from a wrongful act," the attorney for David and Jama told the court in an extraordinary statement that appeared to be convicting Susan of the murder of her husband *before* she had even got to trial.

The Peru Trust Company, the special administrator in the case, received an offer of $155,000 for the house on Summit Drive. It seemed a giveaway price to local real estate brokers who would have happily paid in the region of $250,000 for the property *before* Jim Grund's murder, but then the property did have a certain stigma attached to it. Jimmy's share of Shanty Malone's Bar was sold off for a very modest $15,000.

Then, on April 13, it was announced that Susan's trial date would have to be rescheduled until the following fall. Susan was recovering from a fall inside the Miami County Jail and could not attend the hearing. It emerged that the main reason for the delay in the trial was because a ballistics expert due to be called by Susan's defense attorney, Charlie Scruggs, would be out of the state throughout May, the original date of the trial.

Prosecutor Wil Siders had no objection, but he told the judge, "I only want to try the case once and avoid any error."

On April 15, a court hearing was scheduled in Vincennes to consider a petition to establish new guardians for Susan's two children, Tanelle and Jacob, who had been looked after by their grandmother, Nellie, since their mother's arrest and incarceration.

Jimmy Grund's sister Jane and her husband Fred Allen had decided to seek guardianship of thirteen-year-old Jacob and eight-year-old Tanelle. A two-day hearing was set for June 8 and 9 in Knox County Circuit Court, whose county seat was Vincennes, where Nellie Sanders had fled after the murder of Jimmy Grund.

The Allens decided to seek guardianship after establishing that Jimmy—who had legally adopted the children—had stated in his will that he wanted them to look after the children.

Jane and Fred Allen were at pains to point out that they did not question Nellie Sander's love for her grandchildren, but they genuinely believed they could provide better care for Jacob and Tanelle.

The following month, Susan's attorney Charlie Scruggs suggested that the teddy bear found during the homicide investigation should not be used as evidence in her trial—now scheduled for September, 1993—for the following reasons.

1. An expert firearms witness examined the bear and found no trace of firearms residue.
2. The teddy bear is of no value to the prosecution case so why bother presenting it.

Prosecutor Wil Siders and his team of investigators had still failed to turn up that all important murder weapon and the teddy bear was the nearest thing they had to evidence that Susan hid the gun.

In July, Special Judge Marvin D. McLaughlin, who presided over the hearing to decide whether Susan was entitled to any of the proceeds of the Grund estate, ruled that she was entitled to her one-half interest, regardless of the result of the murder prosecution.

But that distribution of funds—which would have helped Susan begin to pay towards some of her very high legal expenses—was delayed by a motion filed by Grund's son David and daughter Jama Lidral.

Around this time, Susan's mother Nellie rediscovered the metal container that held the gun in the attic of her nephew's home, just before she moved back to Peru from Vincennes. She was surprised because she thought Susan had disposed of it. Nellie decided that she must remember to put it on the U-Haul before her return to Peru. She only wanted to use it as a plant pot. Putrid in color with rotting wooden handles on either end, the boiler had definitely seen better days.

Nellie carefully moved the last box out from the back of the corner of the attic and lifted up the heavy metal container. A few minutes later, she loaded it up with the rest of her stuff and headed back to Peru.

The day after arriving in Peru, Nellie Sanders called the police and told them about the container and what was in it. Her conscience had got the better of her and she couldn't keep quiet about it a moment longer.

As soon as he was told, prosecutor Wil Siders called Gary Nichols at his office on Broadway. "Come on down to Susan's mother's house. I think she's got something for us to look at."

The investigators went equipped with hammers and chisels.

On arrival at the house, Peru Police Sergeant Nichols—Jim Grund's best friend—and Indiana State Police Investigator Bob Brinson struggled to lift the heavy container with its awkward oval shape. Its sides were beaten and dented. It was dirty and old. The investigators started chipping away at the concrete and it gradually began to crumble. There, lying in the bottom was the rusting semiautomatic that had once belonged to David Grund. It was embedded in concrete. They had at last found the key piece of evidence in the murder of Jimmy Grund.

Two aspects of the discovery of the gun really puzzled Nichols, Brinson, and Miami County Prosecutor Wil Siders:

1. Why was there still one bullet from the gun unaccounted for? Susan had started out with thirteen bullets. One was recovered after it exited Jimmy Grund's head, but investigators only ever found eleven. The gun was also in the cocked position. No one could understand why an experienced markswoman like Susan Grund would be so careless.

2. Why did Susan keep the gun after killing her husband? Did she intend to use the gun as a means to prevent David from testifying against her? It was certainly true that at one stage in the investigation the close relationship between Susan and David raised questions for some investigators.

Charlie Scruggs, Susan's defense attorney, was knocked sideways by the news of the discovery of the gun. It was a devastating blow to his defense case. Susan had given him no hint of its whereabouts throughout almost nine months of conversations with her defending counsel.

Up until that point Scruggs had been visiting Susan at least two or three times a week and they had always got along very well. But Scruggs was now beginning to wonder what he had let himself in for.

\* \* \*

Throughout all this, Miami County Prosecutor Wil Siders was determined to retain the right to prosecute the alleged killer of his friend and colleague, Jimmy Grund. Inferences that he was too close to the Grund family were brushed aside—that was Wil Siders's style.

Siders was born forty days earlier than Jim Grund on November 13, 1945, in Miami County, although his slim, athletic build gives a sense of him being younger than his fifty years. Siders has, as he jokingly put it, "four kids of record," and his wife is a nurse. In short, he is yet another member of the same exclusive set that Jimmy Grund belonged to—a man who plays hard and fast, but plays by the book. A prime member of Peru society.

Siders served with the Marine Corps in Vietnam, mainly in Denang. "It gave me a twisted sense of humor when it comes to seeing lots of dead bodies," is his way of explaining away his experiences. He came out of the Marines a captain and soon turned to the law as the best way to earn a good living.

Some observers of the Susan Grund case continued to be rather surprised by Siders's involvement in the case. "Many people thought he was too close to this," said *Peru Daily Tribune* reporter Andy Pierce. But it had long ago become clear that Wil Siders was not going to step down.

Rookie reporter Andy Pierce literally had been thrown in the deep end when he found himself covering the case just a few weeks after joining the paper, following a three-month stint on one of the group's sister papers in nearby Frankfort. Before that Pierce had been at journalism school. At first, the young reporter was flattered that he was being allowed to cover such a prestigious event, until it was pointed out that there was no one else available to do the job. The rest of the *Tribune* staff had been sent out to cover a big drug bust at a house in the country where a new, highly dangerous drug called CAT was being manufactured.

For Pierce, the Grund case was a dream assignment—literally. The twenty-two-year-old reporter rapidly found himself so involved in the story that he started dreaming about developments in the trial before they actually occurred.

An added test for the young scribe was that tape recorders were banned from the courtroom, so he had to use shorthand transcripts which then had to be turned into articles for his paper in double quick time. Peru was proving to have an insatiable appetite for news of the case. Pierce was told by his editor that they had as much space as he could fill each and every day.

Some of the other reporters covering the trial for newspapers in the surrounding areas even had strong personal links with Jimmy Grund and his attractive wife.

Anne Hubbard on the *Kokomo Tribune* had met Jimmy during school board functions she had covered. She had also encountered Susan when she was involved in some of the Miami County pageants. Anne recalled Susan as being very ego oriented and "into herself."

Anne never forgot the day of Jimmy Grund's murder for entirely personal reasons. She had been at the Peru City Park looking for her husband's wedding ring which he had lost the previous day when the call came through that the one-time county prosecutor had been killed. But then most folk in Peru could remember what they were doing on the morning they heard that Jimmy Grund was murdered. It was *that* important of an event.

Back in Peru, Jimmy Grund's ex-wife Jane was completely mystified by the business over the gun and how it had been stolen by Susan from her son David. On numerous occasions following Susan's arrest, she had tried to tackle David about the weapon, but he refused to utter a word about it. Jane presumed it was all just too painful for David to relive. In the end, she completely dropped the subject and it became something that no one dared mention in David's presence.

# Seventeen

With the date of the trial finally approaching, the first task was to pick a jury. Initially, more than eighty potential jurists were interviewed in their home county of Kosciusko County.

The first day of jury selection was not a good day for Susan, though.

As potential jurors were being quizzed by attorneys, they could not fail to notice how sick Susan appeared. As her attorney Charlie Scruggs interviewed them, Susan began fidgeting with a tissue and motioning to her jail matron to take her out of the room.

After she returned, Scruggs continued talking with the potential jurors. At one point, he asked them if they would become "inflated or outraged" if they found out that Susan Grund was having an affair with her husband's son, David.

Prosecutor Wil Siders immediately objected to the question, stating that it transgressed a pretrial agreement that extramarital affairs would not be discussed in court. Intriguingly, the allegations about David

Grund's affair with his stepmother were not apparently intended to be revealed by *either* side in court.

It was becoming increasingly clear that Susan's claims were making the prosecution team feel very uneasy. Why?

Scruggs had in fact made the agreement not to disclose extramarital conduct himself, but only, he later claimed, so that prosecutors could not use such information against his client. Scruggs realized he had to go against his original intentions and make sure Susan's alleged affair with David was discussed in open court, because it was probably the strongest part of his defense strategy.

Scruggs went on to ask jurors if they would be able to give Susan Grund a fair trial once they found out that she had hidden the murder weapon. Some of them soon disqualified themselves through their responses to such questions.

Prosecutor Siders didn't ask too many questions of the pending jurists, except their feelings towards guns. He also asked if they held any religious beliefs that would forbid them from giving Susan a fair trial.

The trial of Susan Grund was being billed in Peru as the county's trial of the century. A steady stream of people flooded into the courthouse from day one as the public gallery was filled to capacity throughout.

Often, people would start lining up outside the building as early as 7:00 A.M. to ensure a good position in one of the court's 156 seats.

To avoid distracting the jury, Special Judge John F. Surbeck, Jr., ordered that no standing would be allowed, and that admittance to the courtroom would only be permitted just before the proceedings began.

The result was vast crowds assembling outside the building every morning.

Spectators were allowed to leave the court at any time, but would not be readmitted until the court recessed. Sheriff Jack Rich even reminded the audience before one lunch break in the first Wednesday of the trial that seating remained "first come, first serve." He said leaving for lunch could mean losing a seat in the courtroom, as there were people waiting outside the courtroom for admittance.

After most lunch breaks throughout the first week of the trial, a double line of people hoping for a seat stretched the length of two sides of the courthouse balcony. Dep. Charles McCord counted an average of seventy-five people standing seatless outside the court each day. He and other sheriff's deputies manned security throughout the case and even operated handheld metal detectors at the court's entrance for fear that somebody might try and take a shot at Susan in the court. Feelings in Peru were running *that* high.

The trial eventually got fully under way on Monday, September 27, 1993.

Susan Grund sat in a not-so-large chair that seemed to envelop her small and thin frame. She sat there, sometimes emotionless, sometimes tearful, sometimes turning her head "no" and showing disagreement with what some witnesses were saying.

One hundred and fifty-six people were watching her every movement, her every mannerism, watching her wipe her eyes and mouth with a Kleenex, watching her turn her head away when pictures of her dead husband were brought before her.

She sat there, pale and sickly, her eyes dark and deep. She looked ill, still suffering from an inner ear infection that seemed to cause her to strain her neck to listen to both testimony and her attorney.

Charlie Scruggs told the jury at the start of the trial that he would attempt to prove his client Susan Grund had an affair with her stepson David Grund, heard him threaten to "get rid" of his father, and then hid the murder weapon.

Prosecutor Wil Siders was greatly worried by this revelation. He immediately sent word to David that he would be expected to give evidence after all. That was something the entire Grund family had been anxious to avoid if at all possible. Now they had no choice. David was going to have to come face-to-face with his stepmother—the woman who claimed he had betrayed his family by carrying out a clandestine affair with her.

Meanwhile, other witnesses were called. First on the stand was Carolyn Shafer, the Dukes Memorial Hospital emergency medical technician who was first at the murder scene. Indiana State Police crime scene technician Dean Marks then appeared and told the court that there seemed to be little evidence of a struggle at the house. Indiana State Police Officer Dennis Trigg, a lab technician at the ISP's base in Lovell, told the court that his examination of the teddy bear didn't find any gunpowder or lead residue inside the toy. But he did testify that when he opened the bear he was able to insert his hand easily and that a gun could have been hidden in the stuffed animal.

When Susan's mother Nellie went on the stand and gave her evidence about finding the container that held the murder weapon, Susan listened intently. But the two women never made eye contact with each other, although Nellie did glance at her daughter a few times. On each occasion, Susan immediately looked away.

Susan and her son Jacob never exchanged one word. The fourteen-year-old walked into the courtroom on Susan's left, passed behind her and took an oath stating he would tell nothing but the truth on the witness stand.

He talked about his mother. He mentioned the arguments between his mother and stepfather and he spoke of what happened on the night Jimmy Grund died. But he never looked, touched, motioned to, or acknowledged the existence of the woman in the courtroom—his mother. He talked about her as a presence, very factually and with little emotion.

Susan watched intently as her stepson David Grund took the stand in the courtroom.

"I never had an affair with that woman," were the first words out of David's mouth.

Susan watched the young man she insisted was her most secret of lovers, with calm disdain. She observed his every movement and there could be no doubt he was well aware of her eyes bearing down on him.

David went on to repeat that he had not slept with his stepmother. The two alleged lovers never once looked directly at each other. David's testimony did not take long. Soon he was gone and others were taking the stand. Perhaps surprisingly, defense attorney Charlie Scruggs did not even attempt to cross-examine David. Two years later, the gritty defense attorney could offer no real explanation why. He simply stated that he did not think it would be in Susan's interests to question David about their alleged affair.

The second day of the trial, a further fifteen people testified, many of them Susan's one-time friends. A lot of them said that she had talked numerous times about having Jim Grund's will changed.

Jim's close friend and business partner Don Bakehorn told the court that Grund had complained to him about Susan constantly talking to him about his will.

Fred Allen—Jim's brother-in-law and partner in the auto dealership—recalled Grund saying that the vacation to Alaska was fine "but Susan was a pain."

Then Susan's sister Darlene's ex-lover Leo Leger admitted upon cross examination that when he was first interviewed by police he pretended he knew nothing about Susan calling by in the early hours of the morning on the way from Vincennes to the house on Summit Drive. He said he had been scared.

"At that time, I didn't want to know anything or remember anything," he told the court. "I figured the least I could say the better."

But then, after talking to a friend involved in law enforcement, Ledger reconsidered and within twenty-four hours gave police a full statement of that encounter with Darlene and Susan on September 3, 1992.

In the early stages of her trial, Susan requested a delay because of her worsening ear infection. She told the court the ear ailment was so painful that she found it increasingly difficult to hear the proceedings. A specialist was then called in. He examined Susan in front of the judge and attorneys, and proclaimed her well enough to continue to stand trial.

The court also heard testimony that showed on the night of Jimmy Grund's death there was a time gap of up to one hour between Susan's travels to her house, Darlene's house, their mother's house, and the reservation campground, where the two boys were due to stay the night.

Then it came to Susan's turn on the stand. The court hushed as she took her position. She had insisted to Charlie Scruggs that she was his best option. This was make or break time.

Under close cross examination from her attorney, Susan went through that last night of Jimmy Grund's life with great precision, talking almost like a third party describing the events from a separate perspective.

But then it came to describing how she claimed she discovered the body.

"I, uh . . . I walked . . . over to him . . . and I saw a gun on the floor . . . and he had a trickle of blood coming out of his mouth. And I, uh, called out to him and there was no answer (sobs). And, uh . . . I touched him . . . (sobs) . . . and, uh, I picked up the gun."

It was a moving display of emotion and it had the jury transfixed. Susan went on to insist she picked up the gun she found alongside the body and took it to the laundry room to hide it.

Q. Why did you do that [hide the gun]?
A. To hide it.
Q. Why did you want to hide it?
A. 'Cause I didn't know what it meant.
Q. What do you mean by that?
A. I didn't know why David's gun would be there.
Q. Was there any other, other reason that you wanted to hide it?
A. 'Cause I had touched it.
Q. Why was that important to you?

A. (Pause) Because once I had touched, I knew that my fingerprints were on it (sobs).

Q. What was significant about that to you?

A. . . . (Sobs) Because if it had done anything to Jim, then, uh . . . (sobs) . . . then I would get blamed for it.

Q. Because your fingerprints were on the gun?

A. Yes.

Q. When you got to the laundry room with the gun, what did you do with it?

A. I hid it in my sewing basket.

Q. Why did you do that?

A. Because I didn't want anyone to see it (sobs).

Q. What was your state of mind at that moment?

A. I just wanted to hurry and hide, and hurry and get him help.

And so the questioning went on. The one question on the minds of the jury was: why, if your husband lay dying in the bedroom, did you not get help instantly instead of worrying about a gun that did not have anything to do with you?

A few minutes later, defense attorney Charlie Scruggs appeared to reduce his client back to tears when he handed her State's Exhibit 3, the gun that killed her husband, and asked her if she had anything to do with the murder.

Susan sobbed instantly and said, "Oh . . . (sobs) . . . no (sobs)."

Shortly afterwards Susan completely broke down when asked by Scruggs to mark an *X* on a photo of the crime scene to show where the gun was in relation to her husband's body when she had found it.

Later, Scruggs dealt adeptly with one of the biggest

holes in Susan's testimony so far—that she had hidden the gun, but not told Trooper Bob Brinson that fact during the interview which occurred just a few hours after the murder of Jimmy Grund.

"I didn't want him to know," insisted Susan to the packed courtroom. "Because I touched it . . . and because I was sure it was David's."

Scruggs then asked, "What significance do you attribute to it being David's gun?"

"I thought he might have had something to do with it," answered Susan to a hushed courtroom. Once again, David Grund's role in his father's death was being questioned.

It was then that Charlie Scruggs decided to lay all his cards on the table.

Q. Okay. Why did you think that David Grund might have had something to do with it?

A. 'Cause they didn't get along.

Q. How do you know that?

A. Because I'm normally the one that had to intervene between their arguments.

Q. What was the problem between the two of them [Jim Grund and his son, David]?

A. Basically, it was finances . . . and . . . and me.

Q. What do you mean about you? What, what was—why was that a problem?

A. Because . . . (sobs) . . . because we'd had an affair.

Q. Who had had an affair?

A. David and I did.

Q. When did that begin and how did it begin?

A. Uh, almost two years prior. One year when Jim went to Canada.

The courtroom was hushed into stunned silence. For the first time in public, details of the alleged affair were about to be discussed.

Susan continued her astonishing testimony. She insisted to the court that the affair with David went on for two years and the love-making became more and more frequent. The summer after their first sexual encounter it increased in regularity because of David's classes. He would come home on a Thursday and then they would spend Fridays together.

And, assured Susan, sex sessions between the couple also took place at the apartment on Main Street where David lived with his girlfriend Suzanne.

Susan insisted she had slept with David the last time in June 1992, less than two months before her husband's murder. Suddenly, this cut-and-dried case was looking a little shaky for prosecutor Wil Siders.

But Susan wasn't finished yet. She also told the court that following a vicious argument with his father, David had said he would "do us both a favor," which clearly implied he was considering killing Jim Grund.

"He said he was gonna get rid of his dad," explained Susan, who claimed that she had ignored the threat as the childish outburst of an irritated young man.

Intriguingly, Susan also testified that on the day of her husband's murder, David called her wanting to know his father's exact movements, saying he had to talk to him urgently.

Susan insisted that David asked her where she was going to be for the remainder of that day. She told him she would not be home because she had to go over to her mother's house. David seemed to want to ensure she was not around.

Susan also claimed that she was under the influence of Valium when she met her sister Darlene and neighbor Mary Pruitt in the dead of night near Indianapolis and made her confession about her role in the murder to Darlene.

She told the court that Darlene had told her to say she killed Jim Grund to protect her stepson/lover David. "I was going to tell them [the police] if I thought it would protect him."

Prosecutor Wil Siders's early interrogation of Susan on the witness stand concentrated on details concerning the day of Jimmy Grund's murder and the July 4 theft of David's gun.

But then he homed in on her alleged affair with her stepson and started to question the validity of her claims. By attempting to pin Susan down on exact dates and times he believed he would then be able to completely discount her story. At one stage, he seemed to be winning when he forced her to commit to a date on which she claimed she was making love to David in the house he shared with Suzanne Plunkett in the country outside Peru. It turned out that David was not even renting the house at the time, although it has to be said that the prosecutor's method of questioning would have confused the most able person.

However, Susan did repeat one very pertinent remark about the phone call she claimed David had made to her at around 5:00 P.M. of the day of Jimmy Grund's murder. She insisted that David told her "not to be around" when he planned to call at the house later that evening.

Next, Siders insisted she again handle the murder weapon in front of the court. Susan mildly took hold of the 9 mm. gun used to kill her husband, grabbed it with less than a full grip and fumbled with it a bit.

She looked at the gun with disgust while Siders asked her to place it on the floor of the Miami County Circuit Court in the same position she found it the night of her husband's murder.

At first, Susan seemed apprehensive, but she then followed Siders's order and placed the gun on the floor, about two and a half feet from a table posing as the couch on which Jim Grund was found dead.

Susan then returned to her seat and fidgeted with a Kleenex tightly wrapped around her left hand as Siders continued his cross-examination.

Susan insisted that both Darlene and her mother were lying when they gave testimony that they did not know about Susan putting the gun in the container which was then filled with concrete.

But the most significant section of Wil Siders's cross-examination came as he asked in very oblique terms whether David Grund was lying when he told the court earlier that he had not had an affair with her.

Q. Are you saying that David Grund is lying to us?
A. About what?
Q. David obviously said he's never had sexual intercourse with you.
A. David's lying.

Siders immediately changed subjects either because he had made his point or perhaps because she was so doggedly sticking to her allegations about an affair with David.

Another strange aspect of Susan's testimony was that she still continued to refer to Indiana State Investigator Brinson as "Bob" despite him being referred to as "Officer Brinson" by everyone else in the court.

Bob Brinson grimaced yet again when he heard her calling him by his first name. It reminded him of those awkward moments of flirtation during that interview just a few hours after Jim Grund's murder.

Wil Siders and his team never revealed Gary Nichols' sky snooping by chopper and later light-plane observation because it might have put them in a bad light. There were many aspects of the case which were never actually disclosed in open court.

One of the most emotional pieces of testimony came from Susan's sister, Darlene.

For Darlene, her court appearance was a terrifying experience. She tried to stay focused on what she had to tell the court by staring at one spot across the room and not glancing in any other direction. But it was plainly obvious to all present that she was very scared.

Darlene recalled how Susan had told her at one stage that she had killed her husband and then panicked because she did not know how to load the gun to shoot herself. "She actually said, 'I shot Jimmy,'" Darlene informed the hushed courtroom. Darlene then told the jury she did not know whether to believe Susan or not.

When asked by prosecutor Wil Siders why, Darlene replied, "She's a liar. She's always been a liar. I thought the whole thing was a lie."

Darlene spoke softly about what her sister had told her that night on September 2 when they went to the house to hide the gun. She sat in the witness chair, twisting a ring on her finger and squeezing her folded hands nervously, barely audible to the jury or the rest of the packed courtroom.

After finishing her testimony, she broke down on the witness stand, red-faced and crying and looked across at Susan for the first time. "Why'd you do it?" she asked.

The last day of the trial began at 9:00 A.M. when prosecutor Wil Siders held up a picture of James Grund, smiling and happy, and then showed a photograph of him on the couch, dead with one bullet through his head.

"Even though many seats in the courtroom are taken, we're still missing one today," he said as he held up the gruesome photograph. "We have a person who is lost here today. That person is Jimmy Grund."

It was a blatantly emotional plea to the jury.

Meanwhile, Charlie Scruggs, for Susan, stated the obvious—that the prosecution was playing on the jury's sympathies.

"And sympathy in a trial is a very dangerous thing," said Scruggs.

The jury retired to consider their verdict shortly afterwards. They looked very concerned about their predicament.

The jurors examined the many photos, statements, reports, and physical evidence from the crime scene and investigation until they departed the courthouse at 6:00 P.M. for a restaurant. At 8:05 P.M., they returned to continue their deliberation.

Judge Surbeck reconvened court at 11:10 P.M. to hear the jury had still not reached a decision. Susan Grund was escorted by law enforcement officers to the courthouse from the Miami County Jail for the proceedings. On her way across Court Street, she was approached by an Indianapolis TV station reporter and cameraman.

The reporter asked Susan how she felt about her

sister testifying against her. Susan did not respond, but looked straight ahead, head held up high in defiance of the journalist's intrusion.

In the courtroom, jury foreman Joe Shoemaker told the judge the jury had voted numerous times and remained split. The jurors had voted 7–5 three times and 10–2 on one occasion, without indicating guilt or innocence in numbers.

Judge Surbeck asked foreman Shoemaker if the jury felt a unanimous decision could be reached today if it adjourned for the night, remaining sequestered and lodged somewhere in the area.

"I honestly don't know," responded Shoemaker.

The judge then recessed the court after asking the jury to retire to the jury room to decide how they wanted to proceed. The 156-strong courtroom audience was allowed to stay seated. Susan sat leaning forward with her head down and her arms crossed.

Fifteen minutes later, Surbeck told the audience in the courtroom that the jury had elected to continue deliberations that night. Sheriff's deputies then asked the audience to leave the courtroom.

Just before Susan Grund was escorted from the courtroom, she smiled and gestured as she talked with her attorney, Charlie Scruggs. But she was repressing untold agonies.

The knots inside Susan's stomach were tied so tight she felt as if she was about to explode. Most nights during the trial she had been literally sick with fear about how the case was progressing. But these last agonizing hours were playing even more havoc with her health.

The twelve jurors and two substitutes walked back into the courtroom looking like war-torn and defeated soldiers returning from the front line. Heads held low, shuffling their feet, the seven women and five men of the jury filed into their selected seats and promptly sat down.

It was 1:25 A.M.—fifteen hours after they first departed to deliberate. Susan Grund watched their expressions closely, tightly holding the hand of her attorney's assistant.

The packed audience sitting in the courtroom sat down in unison in accordance with Judge Surbeck's instructions and an eerie silence filled the courtroom.

When Surbeck asked for the jury's decision, it was clear that they wouldn't be making one tonight—or any other night for that matter.

"We still have several people that won't change their minds. And nobody feels that they could change their minds (with a night's sleep)," explained jury foreman Joe Shoemaker.

Surbeck, looking tired but agreeable, knew there would be no decision. The question remained unanswered—for now.

"Then you are hopelessly deadlocked," he said before declaring a mistrial.

Susan dipped her head into her cupped hands and pressed them upon her eyes. The crowd, unusually quiet, left the courtroom mumbling and with little incident.

It was a hung jury. A tie. In a famous sports phrase, it's like kissing your sister. A non feeling.

"I'm just disappointed, that's all I can say," said Susan's attorney Charlie Scruggs.

On the other side, the opinion was basically the same. "I respect their decision and their frustration, now we go back to square one and start all over again," commented Wil Siders.

The jury members believed that two words were responsible for the disagreement—reasonable doubt.

Significantly, the biggest thing that swayed certain members of the jury to vote "not guilty" was Susan's testimony. They felt they had to give her the benefit of reasonable doubt. Translated into simple terminology it means that many of the jury members believed her allegations about an affair with her stepson, David. It was possible that some of them even believed he might have played a role in the death of his father.

Juror Ned Titus was adamant. "We didn't have the evidence presented to us to put her in this situation. We all felt that she was innocent until proven guilty and we didn't think that it was proven."

Joe Shoemaker insisted, "The prosecution hadn't shown enough evidence to remove the reasonable doubt." The final vote of the jury had been 7–5, not guilty.

The result was like a truism of a forward pass in a football game; three things can occur during a trial and two of them are bad. A mistrial is one of the bad things that happen.

Typically, prosecutor Wil Siders decided to talk to the jury after the verdict to discover what went wrong. He found a jury that was split right down the middle in terms of type; the ones who were overeducated and overpaid just could not believe a respectable woman would commit such a crime while the working "common" people could relate completely to the crime and were convinced of her guilt.

One of the jurors—a seventy-six-year-old woman—even wrote to Wil Siders afterwards to offer her own explanation. In a nutshell, she said, "When you select a jury you want someone who is in touch with reality, someone who has had problems in their life, not someone who has had everything handed to them on a silver platter and cannot relate to something that is bad."

Wil Siders took great note of that letter and decided that whatever happened he was determined to follow that rule when selecting a jury for the next trial.

Meanwhile, Charlie Scruggs believed that although the hung jury had implied that his client was very believable, he was going to face an uphill task at the next hearing because the prosecution now knew all his tactics.

Scruggs believed that he lost the case on the day halfway through the trial, when Susan decided to come to court dressed in a dowdy outfit that hardly befitted that of the sophisticated socialite. In unspoken testimony terms, this was a disaster because it became clear to the jury that she was trying to manipulate them by changing her entire image. It was a huge mistake.

The other problem had been the way that Susan delivered her evidence to the court. It was all so obviously well rehearsed. Whenever Scruggs asked her a question, it was like pressing a button and getting an instant playback. Susan conveyed no *true* feelings or emotion during that testimony.

On cross-examination by Wil Siders, Susan was tactless enough to get angry and raise her voice at the Miami County prosecutor. That was another dreadful mistake. There are two things a defendant should never do; one is don't be a smart-ass and two, don't show anger. Susan had done both.

At that moment, two of the lady jurors had visibly stiffened and leaned back. Scruggs watched and rolled his eyes to the ornate cciling. He reckoned things could only go downhill from then on.

# Eighteen

Just days after the first trial had ended in a hung jury in November, Susan's defense attorney Charlie Scruggs announced he was formally asking the Miami Circuit Court to allow him to withdraw from his position.

Three days later, Susan Grund found herself sitting alone at the large defense table in the courtroom to discuss Scruggs's request with Judge Surbeck and Wil Siders.

Susan even made a motion to the judge confirming that Scruggs had received "grossly inadequate attorney's fees." The motion also stated that Scruggs had received just $3,000 for expenses, but had incurred over $6,000 in actual court litigation expenses.

The following month, Charlie Scruggs climbed back on board the Susan Grund defense team and tried his hardest to get his client released on bail. Scruggs had returned to Susan's side after an arrangement had been made whereby he could be paid his fees for the first trial.

Once back in charge, Scruggs claimed that Susan had a constitutional right to bail because seven out of the twelve jurors found her not guilty. But the judge denied the motion.

A few weeks after the end of the first trial, Jim Grund's sister Jane got a telephone call from Susan, still incarcerated in the Miami County Jail in Peru. She wanted to talk to her children, Tanelle and Jacob.

"Are they there?" asked Susan coldly.

She then struggled to talk to Jacob and Tanelle, who barely responded to her inane conversation. Eventually, the call ended ten minutes earlier than the time she had been allotted by the jail. Her role as their parent seemed to be over.

For the wasted lives and bartered souls that were making time at the Peru County Jail, it was the incessant echoing that dictated the mood of the place. More regular than a heartbeat, the eerie dark noise of voices reached into the viscera and pulled your poor helpless volition into alignment with the sweaty fear and rage that undermined the atmosphere in that clean-as-a-hospital-operating-room jail. The echoes were like the soundtrack to the endless hours of boredom, straining under the endless, oppressive hours, minutes, and seconds that strung together to finally mark the passing of another day. That distant echoing gave voice to a dark reality of the human spirit that polite society had isolated behind those eight-inch-thick walls.

Inside Miami County Jail, Susan Grund was considering her fate. Was this second trial an opportunity for justice or just another foregone conclusion?

Early-rising Miami County residents intent on exercise opened their doors in February 1994 to a gloomy, chillingly cold dawn, a rude introduction to the beginning of between-the-seasons weather that was too cold for spring, but not cold enough to pass for winter.

But before Susan's second murder trial could begin, another careful jury selection had to be carried out. And a decision was made to hold the trial at the Kosciusko County Court in Warsaw, Indiana, because it seemed a more objective location than back to the "lion's den" in Peru. The judge also felt that the vast crowds at the first trial were hardly conducive to a fair hearing. In Warsaw, there was a smaller courtroom, which meant less room for the sort of drama that filled the first trial.

Tighter crowd control and security was a top priority. Smoking was also banned from the entire first and second floors to avoid the complaints of excessive smoking during the first trial.

Three at a time, prospective jurors were escorted into the Kosciusko County Court; teachers, homemakers, business owners, retirees, hospital workers, the unemployed—they were all there. Then they were asked questions by Wil Siders and Charlie Scruggs. Susan showed little emotion as she assisted Scruggs in the selection, her hair pulled back in a neat and glamorous fashion with a sweater draped over her shoulders.

Susan, still apparently suffering ear problems, labored to listen to what was said in court and had to turn her neck almost completely around to hear what Scruggs, sitting to her left, said.

He asked questions to determine the jurors' ideas on justice. Questions to see how logical they were. Questions to see if they had been tainted by the media coverage of the case.

"All I'm asking for is twelve people who know nothing about this case and are willing to give their one-hundred-percent attention to the case at hand," Siders told the prospective jurors. "All I want you to do is promise not to make a decision until all the facts are in."

Charlie Scruggs later reiterated Siders's remarks, asking the potential jurors if they felt that rendering a not guilty verdict was as important as rendering a guilty verdict, when discussing the concept of justice.

All answered simply, "Yes."

But still some were not chosen. Scruggs also asked the jurors if they would give Susan Grund a fair trial even if she admitted to hiding the murder weapon and having a sexual affair with her stepson, David—an affair he has always strenuously denied.

All answered simply, "No."

This was a significant reaction because Scruggs based his most controversial decision of both hearings on that response; he stopped Susan from repeating her allegations about having sex with David in the second trial because he was afraid it might prejudice her case. Scruggs felt it would work against the interests of his client. In other words, she did not discuss the subject on Scruggs' advice. Susan was angry about this decision because it made her feel as if she was retracting her claims of an affair with David made during the first trial. In fact, Susan still continued in private to insist the affair *did* happen, but she had no choice at her second trial as she had to take the advice of her attorney. It was a decision she later bitterly regretted.

Back at the jury selection session at the Kosciusko County Court in Warsaw, the two attorneys were finding it much harder to pick a good jury than at the first trial the previous September.

About halfway through the proceedings, one potential juror told the court she had been tainted by reading a story in the Sunday *Fort Wayne Journal-Gazette* and that others in the waiting room had been talking about the case.

Judge Surbeck then called the rest of the potential jurors into the courtroom to ask them to refrain from speaking about the case while waiting to be questioned by the attorneys.

"I know that when people get together and have nothing else to talk about these things happen," Surbeck told the group. "But we ask that each of you refrain from commenting on what you think of the case."

Many of those chosen to sit on the panel gave the perfect answers when discussing open-mindedness and innocence and the need to be proven guilty. But the two attorneys did agree on one juror who admitted to knowing one of the proposed witnesses, Zoyla Henderson, owner of Peru's finest bed-and-breakfast establishment, Rosewood Manor.

Henderson had testified during the first trial that Susan once said her job in life was "to set up Jim so well that if he ever left me he'd leave with nothing."

In a surprising admission, the same juror even admitted to reporters after the selection hearing that she knew things about both Henderson and Susan Grund that "would color my judgment of her." But the woman remained a juror.

In all, eighty jurors were called during jury selection on March 7 and March 8, 1994. They were paid a modest twenty-five cents a mile from their homes to the Kosciusko County Courthouse. They were also paid $17.50 a day if not chosen and $35 a day if chosen.

At the end of the trial, it emerged that the county had spent $7,692.21 on jury expenses alone. The judge himself was on $25 a day and twenty-five cents a mile. He also received meals and free lodging.

There was also another reason for switching courtrooms to Warsaw. The jurors would have easier freedom of movement to come and go without actually having to step through the crowds. Authorities believed that this might make the jury feel less intimidated by the occasion.

Throughout the second trial, people got frustrated with the long wait to get in the courtroom because of the smaller audience capacity. But authorities refused to change the location. Everything was being done this time to ensure a fair trial for Susan Grund.

For Susan herself, this trial did not seem so frightening. She had been there before. She had sat in court and listened to Wil Siders call her a murderer. She had sat in court and listened to Charlie Scruggs try to defend her. She had sat in court before and watched the reactions of the jury sitting in judgment on her. The only difference was that this time the case was being heard at the Kosciusko County Courthouse.

Susan did look directly at the jurors without expression when the charge of murder against her was read to the full panel for the first time. But from that moment on there was a look of blankness on her face. She could do nothing more than sit back and listen.

Most of the arguments and testimony used in the first trial were wheeled out once more. Prosecutor Wil Siders referred to "the tangled web we are going to weave." He was even using the same notes he had in front of him throughout the first trial.

But this time Siders preempted any potential bombshell disclosures like Susan's alleged affair with David in the first trial, by getting in the first mention of her claims of illicit sex with her stepson.

"David is nothing more than another lie," insisted Siders.

Susan watched him say those words with a desperate sense of frustration. She so wanted to tell the world about the affair, but she had been told not to mention it by Charlie Scruggs.

Defender Charlie Scruggs insisted, "Things are not always what they appear." He said that Susan had used "very, very bad judgment" when she picked up the murder weapon, but she did not shoot her husband.

And he told the jury, "Don't convict on a suspicion of guilt. Keep in mind the thing is not always what the facts appear to be. Listen and apply your common sense. We want to find out the truth here."

Scruggs fervently believed that the prosecution was going to use Susan's claims of an affair with David as further evidence against her. They would try and convince the jury that her theft of David's gun made even more sense because of her infatuation. In other words, *hell hath no fury like a woman scorned.* Or at least that was how the prosecution intended to turn around the case if Susan repeated her claims.

Charlie Scruggs was absolutely correct. Wil Siders did indeed plan to use Susan's claims of an affair as further evidence of her premeditated murder scheme. Clearly, he believed that she was trying to frame David for his father's killing because he had either ended the affair or turned down Susan's attempts to begin a relationship in the first place.

One of the numerous holes in the prosecution case

emerged when Indiana State Police Sgt. Gary Boyles conceded that David Grund could have taped all the TV programs the night of his father's death and that would explain why he so impressed the investigator with his detailed knowledge of the shows he claimed he watched when he stayed in that entire evening. But this weak aspect of the prosecution case was never fully exploited by the defense team.

Dr. Dean Gifford, the pathologist who carried out the autopsy on Jim Grund in the early hours of August 4, 1992, even testified that he could not deny that there was a possibility Grund did commit suicide.

"My opinion is that this was a homicide," Gifford told the court. "It's unusual for a person to shoot himself in the eye, usually it's either in the mouth or temple . . . but there's no way to know one hundred percent."

When David Grund took the stand, he was asked detailed questions by Wil Siders about his movements on the night of his father's murder because there was still the faintest cloud of suspicion hanging over his involvement in the killing.

David insisted that he had eaten that night at his girlfriend Suzanne's parents' house before going home to watch television. He told the court that he and Suzanne went to bed around 11:00 P.M.

Yet again, Susan's attorney Charlie Scruggs did not attempt to cross-examine David. Two years later he insisted there was no point in doing so.

Back in court that day, Charlie Scruggs did win a small victory when he persuaded the judge not to allow the prosecution to talk about Susan's previous marriages and her "bad acts in the past."

"Just because a person has a bad marriage doesn't

mean they're likely to kill their spouse," insisted Scruggs. "It's extremely prejudicial."

The judge agreed and told the court, "The defendant's character is not admissible until he or she puts it in. If you have direct evidence of their marriage within a reasonable period of time then we'll talk about letting that be in, but I'm not going to allow any character assassinations. That's not going to happen."

When Susan's sixty-two-year-old mother, Nellie Sanders, gave evidence, Susan just sat there, staring straight ahead. She was emotionless despite the fact this was the woman who raised her, fed her, clothed her, and sheltered her.

Later, Susan's sister Darlene took the stand and repeated her account of what happened. Then Wil Siders decided to take issue with any forthcoming defense suggestions that Darlene was somehow out to get revenge on her prettier, younger sister.

Siders asked Darlene. "Is it a fair statement that you love your sister?"

"Yes," replied Darlene. She was clearly close to tears. She looked over in the direction of Susan, who did not even bother to lift her head and acknowledge the glance.

Charlie Scruggs later insisted to the court that Darlene was a liar who was "evasive and vague." He pointed out that Darlene could almost be considered an accessory to the murder.

One of Susan's other sisters, Rita Saylors, backed Scruggs by insisting to the court that Darlene was not a reliable witness. The case had well and truly split Susan's family apart. Rita later insisted that her sister had been having an affair with David and she believes her sister was the victim of a complete miscarriage of justice.

Throughout the early stages of the second murder hearing, Susan sat without uttering a word to the court. She occasionally exchanged looks with family members seated in the back row of the courtroom and made brief comments into the ear of her attorney.

Susan finally took the stand herself on March 13. She looked a slight figure, dressed in black, turning slightly to face the jury who were to decide if she was guilty of murdering her husband. Sometimes, she would stare directly at them with disturbing and relentless eyes. She rarely looked at Wil Siders or even her attorney, Charlie Scruggs, whom she clearly resented by this stage.

Susan was growing increasingly upset by the restrictions placed on her by Scruggs, even turning and saying to the jury at one stage that, "It's difficult when you're confined as to what you can say."

Her voice was high, light, shaky, and nearly impossible to discern at times, but she still managed to convey confidence in her story.

The only real change in Susan's testimony from her first trial came when she told the court that she did in fact pick up her dog from her mother's house on the night of the murder. Earlier, she had claimed the dog had stayed at her mother's until the following day.

Susan became highly emotional when Wil Siders forced her to examine a photograph of the death scene, featuring a very gruesome picture of her dead husband.

"No," she screamed. "Take that away." She then broke down crying on the witness stand for about two minutes.

After she had regained her composure, Susan insisted to the court, "I never saw him like that. Never!"

For a total of three hours and five minutes, Susan

defended herself against over fifteen hours of testimony the prosecution had piled up against her.

Later, as she told of the events of August 3, 1992, the day her husband was killed, she repeated her predicament, "How can I tell them . . . there's so much I can't say. I can't repeat conversations."

Significantly, Charlie Scruggs even sided with prosecutor Siders when he agreed that she should not keep making such remarks to the court.

Susan was clearly upset and angry, even when the judge threatened to call another mistrial and reconvene in six months, if she did not stop attempting to tell the jury that there were things she could not say. But that was the key to Susan's frustration—there clearly were things she wanted to tell the jury, but couldn't.

"I thought I had a right to explain things?" Susan snapped back at Judge Surbeck.

Prosecutor Wil Siders later asked Susan's mother if she would come back to the witness stand to refute some of her daughter's testimony. After doing so, Nellie Sanders did not leave the courtroom as she should have. She looked over towards Susan, who was quietly sobbing into her Kleenex.

Nellie then slowly walked over to Susan, leaned over the table her crying daughter was sitting behind, and said, *"I love you, honey, more than you'll ever know."*

Then she walked out.

The judge then allowed prosecutor Wil Siders to present his final nail in Susan's coffin: a line-up of local dignitaries who were prepared to tell the court what an untruthful person Susan was. Charlie Scruggs and his client knew that this was most probably the beginning of the end.

1. First came Judge Bruce Embrey. "I do not consider her to be a truthful person. Her reputation within the community is very poor."
2. Then followed Jack Vetter, the Florida businessman who provided the boat that Jimmy and Susan married on. "I don't think she's a very honest person."
3. Don Bakehorn, Jimmy Grund's business partner in Shanty Malone's and one of the wealthiest people in Peru. "Susan is not a truthful person."
4. Jimmy Grund's sister Jane Allen. "She's a liar."
5. Betty Crawshaw, wife of Jimmy's friend Dr. John Crawshaw. "She lies. She's not to be believed."

And so it went on. The issue of Susan's so-called dishonesty was made loud and clear by the first witness, but Wil Siders decided to keep ramming the point home over and over again.

During summing up, Siders told the jury that Susan was a woman with no job skills, a woman who was on her fourth marriage. "If ever you have a character you can characterize as a gold digger, this is it."

But Charlie Scruggs concentrated on the testimony of her sister Darlene Worden. He told the jury that Darlene had every reason to lie because she was afraid of being charged as an accessory. "Darlene Worden is not credible. She's not worthy of belief."

Scruggs rounded off his summing up by insisting, "I don't know who could have done this. A prosecuting attorney has many enemies. A lawyer makes enemies. We're not here for vindictive justice. Let's get the right person."

The jury deliberation had included an examination of ninety pieces of evidence. The jurors had listened to fifty-one witnesses during the four days of testimony in the second trial.

When the jury finally went out, Susan began the anxious wait for a verdict that was witnessed by all those present in that crowded courtroom.

She stood against the railing that divided her from the packed audience for much of the time. Occasionally, she would hold the hand of her attorney's assistant, Stephanie Doran. Sometimes, a tear would appear to stream slowly down her cheek. She dabbed at it with a tissue. Eventually, those solitary tears turned into a veritable flood of emotion, but it was difficult to tell whether this was the real Susan or simply an image she wished to portray to the court.

On March 23, 1994, following a midnight notice from the jury, Special Judge Surbeck of Allen Superior Court reconvened court. Susan had her blonde hair pushed back off her pretty, angular face by a thick black band which made her look like one of those stern-faced B-movie starlets of the fifties. It had been thirteen hours and thirty-five minutes since they had departed to consider their verdict. Most of them took a brief peek at the woman charged with murdering her husband as they filed back into the courtroom. In each case, it was purely a cursory glance.

The judge then asked the jury foreman if a decision had been reached.

"Yes," replied the foreman. He then passed a written statement to Judge Surbeck. The judge hesitated then read a formal verdict: "Guilty."

Friends and family in the court exclaimed "Yes" and "There is a God" in an instantaneous burst of reaction as Susan Grund buried her anguished face into her fists and handkerchief without a sound. Then, almost just as many of the crowd began to weep. Her mother, her sister, her friends. They recognized the tragedy that had unfolded in front of their very eyes. It was a tragedy that could so easily have been avoided.

Surbeck then asked each juror—all of them were Kosciusko County residents—directly by name if the decision announced was correct. Almost simultaneously, Susan began to cry, her eyes pleading in their direction as she wept.

"Yes, sir," was echoed by the ten women and two men of the jury.

Surbeck thanked the jurors for their service and attention and excused them from the courtroom. Later, he thanked Scruggs and Siders for their work.

Surbeck ordered a tentative sentencing date of 10:00 A.M. on April 15. He warned there could be changes in the date and time if either the prosecution or defense had a conflict. None of this mattered to Susan; she rubbed her eyes and quietly continued to sob. She faced a prison term of thirty to sixty years, but it really didn't matter anymore.

After court was recessed, Susan was hurriedly escorted out of the courtroom with Charlie Scruggs. On one side of her was Sheriff Jack Rich. On the other, his wife, jail matron Linda Rich. They were both solemn faced in the glare of the television lamps and popping flashbulbs. They even looked as if they felt a twinge of sympathy for their star prisoner.

Linda Rich held Susan's arm in a motherly fashion as Susan tried desperately to turn away from the cameras. Her head was bowed; an immaculate white lace handkerchief clutched up to her face hiding either those emotionless eyes or maybe a genuine tear or two. It was hard to tell. The photos that appeared in the newspapers next day certainly helped project the image of a woman who might actually have felt sorry for what she was alleged to have done.

Some of Susan's friends in the public gallery for the second trial also could not help feeling great sympathy for Susan—despite that cold, heartless image. Local journalist Nancy Newman, who knew Susan's retarded brother and her father, as well as regularly encountering the "classy" version of Susan once she had married Jim Grund, actually felt for her friend. She and others believed that Susan's biggest mistake had been her unashamed ambition to get to the right side of the tracks. Now she was paying the ultimate price.

Back in the courtroom, prosecutor Wil Siders was speaking to the jury and thanking them profusely for their time and effort.

After the trial, Siders hinted at so-called shocking stories about Susan's personal life that were never brought before the jury. Why? Was it because of some inbuilt sensitivity on the part of the hard-nosed prosecutor? Or was it because Susan Grund's dirty linen might well have involved a number of familiar figures from Peru's elite, ruling class? We shall never know.

Even Wil Siders admitted after the hearing, "If there was any mistake and if anyone made one it should be looked at very carefully." But he, along with all the other law officers involved in the case, had no intention of raking over old ground. Privately, Siders was a very relieved man. He knew that Susan probably would have got away with murdering her husband if she had not told anyone about what she had done.

The moment she confided in her sister Darlene, her fate was sealed.

Jimmy Grund's father, James A. Grund, was quietly happy about the verdict, although nothing was going to bring back his son. However, the wily old lawyer did make one very significant comment: "We did the best job we could for him to avenge his murder." For revenge was a very clear motive in the two trials of Susan Grund.

James Grund decided there and then that whatever happened, the eternal flame burning over his son's grave would remain burning forever as a lasting tribute to one of the county's finest citizens—Jimmy Grund.

# Nineteen

Following the trial, local journalists were promised that Susan would hold a press conference. The Grund family were horrified by any such plan as they did not want Susan to get any more coverage for her crime. Then the press conference got mysteriously cancelled. Some reporters believed the Grund family managed to put a halt to the plan, while others reckoned that Susan was advised by her attorney not to speak publicly for fear it might not help her when it came to her sentencing hearing the following month.

Many local people and journalists remain convinced that the key to the case lay with Susan's claims of an affair with her stepson, David Grund. Many insisted there was a relationship and numerous Peru citizens had been hoping that a press conference by Susan might help clear the air.

"Some of what she said was pretty convincing. David was a shaky sort," commented the *Peru Daily Tribune*'s young star reporter, Andy Pierce. "The way Susan described them being in bed together, hearing

Jimmy in the garage coming in, the bed being messed up. It was believable. He was a good looking kid."

Naturally, journalists were also keen to interview David Grund. But he remained as tight-lipped as ever, under strict family instructions not to talk to anyone publicly about the case.

Some locals pointed out that the *Peru Daily Tribune* had definite ties to the Grund family. The President of the corporation which owned the newspaper lived near Jimmy and Susan, on Summit Drive.

Reporter Andy Pierce also noted that he was instructed not to lean on the Grund family. "I was always told to give the family as much room as possible and we were not to approach them except at the end of the trial for a brief comment."

The following day, the local radio station was swamped with requests for songs with titles that bore some relation to the conviction. The tracks chosen included, "Devil Woman," "Run Around Sue," "Poison Ivy," "Working on the Chain Gang," "Evil Woman," "Indiana Wants Me," "Take these Chains from my Heart," "Rescue Me," "Money Can't Buy Me Love," and so on. Every time one came on a cheer could be heard in some corner or other of Peru.

Susan's attorney Charlie Scruggs faced a barrage of criticism from his client following his decision not to allow her to talk about her alleged affair with David at the second trial.

But Scruggs genuinely believed the prosecution would have so many other lovers of Susan's on standby that reference to her alleged affair with her stepson would weaken his defense, rather than strengthen it. He has never been able to fathom whether the relationship occurred or not, "only David and Susan know the truth."

After the case, David Grund was rarely seen in Peru. He and girlfriend Suzanne moved up to Michigan where David was attending a local law school.

Susan's friend Mary Heltzel got a letter from Susan on March 24, 1994. She was still in the Miami County Jail awaiting sentencing at the time.

Susan wrote, "The shock is wearing off and the realization of the verdict is sinking in. I will never understand how Mother and Darlene can live with themselves. But knowing Darlene she will."

Susan clearly intended to appeal the verdict and fight on. She went on, "Jim is my husband and he would never approve of what his family did or what has happened to me or our children. The Grunds know this too. He is not resting in peace and I will fight because he would have."

Susan seemed angry about Charlie Scruggs's representation of her.

Her seething anger about Darlene and her mother had grown even stronger over the months. "I don't know how they can live with themselves."

Susan then revealed that she planned on going to school once she got to the state prison because school helps to reduce your sentence. "But we are still praying for a miracle," she wrote.

Less than two weeks later, another letter showed up at Mary's home. This time, Susan mentioned school again, obviously it was becoming a real obsession for her. She was also looking forward to being allowed to wear her own clothes in state prison.

In reference to a male relative of Mary's who had

just been imprisoned, Susan wrote, "Men's prison is nothing like women's. But women's is bad enough."

On April 15, 1994, Susan appeared in court once again to hear her sentence passed for murdering her husband, Jimmy Grund. As she sat in the Miami County Courthouse where pictures of her husband's grandfather, Circuit Judge Hurd J. Hurst, and his uncle, fellow Circuit Judge Frank Dice, hung from the walls, she knew that her battle was over.

This time Susan did not testify on her own behalf. Charlie Scruggs advised her not to say anything because it might make the judge even harsher on her when it came to sentencing.

Special Judge Surbeck of nearby Allen County did not pull any punches when he described Susan as cold and calculating. He also made a point of mentioning that during her second trial the jury convicted her quickly, implying that was significant evidence in regard to her guilt.

"You have to have calmly, coldly and calculatedly carried it out and then returned to your children," Surbeck told Susan in front of a hushed courtroom. "There is also premeditation there because you either stole the gun or had it stolen from, of all people, the victim's son."

Judge Surbeck insisted there were no mitigating circumstances, and that a number of aggravating circumstances had led him to decide on the harshest sentence possible. The most relevant event of all was the no-contest plea Susan made in 1983 in Oklahoma, following those awful child battery accusations.

Then photographs of her bruised, bloodied and severely sunburned stepson, Tommy Whited, appeared on a slide projector screen in the Miami County Court. The packed room gasped in horror.

Oklahoma City Police Det. J. M. Einhorn took the stand and glanced coldly across at the woman he last met as she tried to defend her actions in beating a child close to death more than ten years earlier. He then explained to the court quietly, "The only way Tommy can eat now is through a hole in his stomach."

Susan's attorney Charlie Scruggs valiantly attempted to water down the impact of Susan's child battery case by having ten witnesses appear on her behalf before sentencing. Most of them were only on the stand for about a minute each and many of them spoke of her good work for the Miami County 4-H Fair.

But those words were soon forgotten when the Grund family got their say. All six family members told the court they wanted Susan to get the maximum sentence. Emotion-filled testimony about Jimmy Grund's links with the law and the town of Peru made it sound more like a public obituary than a sentencing in a court of law.

There was much talk about Susan possibly selling her story to the media and the Grunds had something to say about that subject as well. They insisted she should not profit from the murder of Jimmy Grund.

Prosecutor Wil Siders—friend and colleague of the Grunds for more than twenty years—made a point of commenting, "The value of her story went down immensely after she was found guilty. One would presume that she told the truth on the stand so if she tried to sell a different story, who would believe it?" There was an understandable amount of glee in his voice.

Members of the Grund family also related conflicts

and lies attributed to Susan Grund and requested the maximum sentence. Their feelings were expressed in person and by handwritten notes addressed to "Dear Judge Surbeck."

David Grund—the young man whom some in Peru still believe to this day had a sexual liaison with his stepmother—tearfully stated that Susan "does not deserve to live. But since the law does not allow the death penalty, we cannot afford to not give her the maximum penalty."

The Judge responded by telling the court that Susan's criminal history showed a refusal to conform to society's rules and a propensity for violence. He even predicted rather gloomily that "the likelihood of rehabilitation is slim."

He awarded the standard sentence of forty years with an additional twenty years for aggravating circumstances. Susan was also fined $10,000, the maximum allowed by law. It seemed strange to those present that she should face a cash penalty. It was almost as straightforward as a parking violation ticket.

Immediately after the sentencing, Susan was transported to the women's prison in Indianapolis by the Miami County Sheriff's Department. She had served 529 days since her arrest on November 3, 1992, and would not be eligible for parole until the year 2024, by which time she will be in her midsixties.

Peru's upper-class citizens were delighted by the sentence and decided to celebrate Susan's imprisonment in style. Dozens of local dignitaries attended a celebration party at Shanty Malone's that same evening.

Jimmy Grund's rich and influential friends even had a T-shirt specially printed up to commemorate Susan the murderer. Oklahoma City Det. J. M. Einhorn—who had brought Susan to trial on those child battery charges—had never seen anything like it before in his life. The whole town seemed to be partying.

The T-shirts were strictly limited edition. Wil Siders kept one. Gary Nichols gave his to Einhorn. They were grey in color and they featured a cartoon about the sentencing. None of the investigators would produce one for anyone to see, so the contents remain a secret to this day.

The party at Shanty Malone's was quite a wild affair by all accounts. Jimmy Grund's elderly mother Connie got so merry she ended up dancing on the bar. Jim Grund's great friend Sgt. Gary Nichols even managed to pat her rear end in the process. Judge Surbeck and his attractive wife joined in the spirit of the occasion and everyone held nonstop toasts to various investigators involved in the case.

Wil Siders held one very private toast in the corner of Shanty Malone's that night. For he believed there was one unsung hero in this entire saga—Susan's sister, Darlene. It would have been easy for her to sit back and say nothing about what her sister had told her. But she came forward and contributed more than any other individual to her sister's arrest. Siders held a silent tribute to Darlene. Without her, he would never have got that conviction.

Shortly after the end of the second trial, Susan's defense attorney Charlie Scruggs announced he would not be representing her in any appeal she planned to make against her conviction.

Scruggs insisted that his client had, in his opinion, received a fair trial, and he did not feel he could go any further with her case. Scruggs also pointed out that virtually every murder conviction gets appealed by the defendant.

An appeal by Susan would not automatically guarantee her a new trial, but it would allow the Indiana Supreme Court to examine court records to see if any legal errors were made that pointed toward an unfair trial.

But Charlie Scruggs made a damning indictment of her case by saying, "I think she got a fair trial. I don't think any mistakes were made and I don't think an appeal would be successful. I felt Susan received the due process of law and a fair trial. She will have to live with the verdict and suffer the consequences of that."

What Charlie Scruggs did not make a point of mentioning was that although he received payment for his services during the first trial, he did not receive a penny for his work on the second hearing.

Susan eventually hired a deputy state public defender called David Freund to handle her appeal. At the time of writing, Freund had just received an extension for the appellate brief.

After sentencing, Susan was given a thirty-day period of no contact while adjusting to her new home at the Indiana Women's Prison, near Indianapolis. She was all alone and away from Peru for the first time since her arrest.

Mary Heltzel received a letter from Susan after her sentencing. This time the envelope had Susan's impressive personalized name and address on a gold sticker. It was only possible to tell it was from a prison by the initials "I.W.P." on the address tag.

Susan had sent an expensive Christmas card with a carefully typed note to Mary and her family. The card was signed, "Sending you my very best for the holiday season, Much Love, Susan."

Intriguingly, the enclosed note was clearly a copy of something Susan had sent to all her friends and family with a seasonal greeting card.

Susan's studies in criminal justice in prison were going well. Her health had improved with the exception of a few minor setbacks. She continued enjoying singing in the jail choir and regularly appeared in Christmas concerts. Susan's weekly Bible study classes were also going very well. She also completed all three parts of a correspondence Bible study course.

Susan was in many ways thriving on prison life. She taught other inmates makeup and beauty tips and she commanded a certain level of respect through her alleged crimes, which had elevated her to the status of a star prisoner. Her obsession with religion continued and she wrote to her friend Mary, "I may not be able to move the mountains but my faith in GOD and HIS ability to move the mountains will reach HIM through prayers. I hope that you pray for the grave concerns and needs as we can all use all the prayers to see us through."

Near Valentine's Day, on February 9, 1995, Mary received a card from her friend Susan. In it, Susan made clear she was still hinging everything on her eventual appeal. She wrote, "The attorneys are still moving too slow but at least they are moving. . . ."

Susan's mother Nellie and sister Darlene have not spoken to her for more than two years. She has even refused to reply to their letters. Her sprightly sixty-three-year-old mother also firmly believes that more people than just Susan were involved in the killing of Jimmy Grund.

She talks in dramatic terms about gun running, drug dealing, dog and rooster fighting and even white slavery going on behind the respectable doorways of the tightly knit community of Peru.

In early 1995, Nellie claimed she received a number of threatening phone calls to her rundown home on East 3rd Street, in the center of town.

The callers refer to "one dead and two more to go and you're one of them." Nellie says it's a muffled voice. She believes that she knows too much about her daughter's case and, "I ain't afraid to tell no one. . . ."

Meanwhile, Susan Grund continued to harbor a deep resentment for everyone involved in her arrest and subsequent trial. She felt she was the victim rather than the perpetrator of that horrendous crime.

Murder had not erased or changed the past because she hated everyone even more than she did before the climax of all that emotion ended in Jimmy Grund's death. Even during the course of her alleged crimes, she found that it was only her own confused background that was being acted out by that ultimate act of violence. She had failed yet again. No real power could be achieved and Susan was feeling empty, forlorn, and damned as she had throughout the entirety of her troubled life. By committing a murder, she had simply reinforced all her own convictions. She had become the victim now because she remained unfulfilled and unsatisfied. Not even the huge banner headlines were enough to help her recapture the power she had once enjoyed.

For months after her sentencing she fed off her own sorrow. All the while she was going about life in jail, as if it were normal on the surface. She remained lucid, but it was expected that the fantasies would eventually return and then she would feel the need to get more revenge.

Back in Peru, Susan's sister Darlene is still riddled with guilt over the testimony she gave against Susan in court.

"I feel torn up about telling on my sister. It has split the family up real bad. I would not have done it if I had known. Nobody in all this is entirely blameless. I don't think Susan is innocent, but there were other forces at work. I have no doubt about that."

Darlene stopped all communications with her sister when she threatened to try and implicate her mother in the hiding of the gun that was used to murder Jimmy Grund.

"You make your bed you lay in so don't be dragging someone else into your mess," is Darlene's interpretation of that situation.

It seems that Susan Grund's bed is permanently made. . . .

# Afterword

There was not so much an ending as a final turning point in this complex story. The horrible events unleashed by Susan Grund left indelible marks upon everyone who came into contact with her. They seemed to have a dual need to see Susan behind prison walls for the rest of her life and to return to normalcy. The second could not be realized until the first was accomplished.

Then there was Susan Grund's most tragic victim: her stepson, Tommy Whited.

Even Jimmy Grund's elderly mother, Connie Grund, believed that, despite losing her own son, little Tommy was the most heartbreaking of Susan's victims.

"He never had a chance. She just battered the life out of him before he could even begin to appreciate life. . . ."

Oklahoma City District Court Judge Charlie Weir has been haunted by the case ever since he tried it back in 1983. He believes to this day that it was something that should never have happened.

Usually in child abuse cases, there is unemployment, financial deprivation, and a general breakdown of home life as we know it. But with Tommy, the family appeared to be intelligent, fairly well-off people.

Judge Weir remembered the father as a fine-looking man and Susan as an attractive woman. But something inexplicably so frustrated Susan that she was driven to inflict that awful abuse on her stepson.

Almost as inexplicable was Tommy's father's failure to react to his son's injuries.

"How could he not have noticed his child was being abused?" asked Judge Weir more than ten years later.

"Life is not fair, and perhaps we shouldn't expect it to be fair. But that doesn't make it any easier, does it?

"I signed the order that terminated Tommy's father's parental rights to him. But it doesn't really affect the really important things, does it?"

Det. J. M. Einhorn, the solid, hardworking Oklahoma cop who also never forgot the evil mother whom he helped prosecute for child battery, described the sentencing of Susan Grund for her husband's murder as "Tommy's day."

Meanwhile, little Tommy remains in a children's convalescent center in Bethany, Oklahoma. His care is continuing to be provided for by his natural mother's father, Lester Suenram.

One of Tommy's hands remains in a curled, fixed position due to his mental retardation and the after-effects of his medication to curb seizures. He can only volunteer one coherent word—food.

Tommy is not even able to support himself properly

in a chair so he is moved around in a specially adapted wheelchair with a handmade curved back to fit the shape of his spine, which has curved because he has spent so much time in bed. He has a tray on his chair. But he cannot put anything in his hands because he cannot hold on for more than a few seconds.

Lester Suenram has spent a small fortune ensuring that Tommy is properly looked after. He built a new wing on his house after Tommy was originally released from hospital back in 1983. Then Lester himself suffered a stroke and the boy was transferred to the convalescent center.

They say Tommy looks a lot like his father. But his mouth is always bone dry and he needs tubes to be properly fed. The dried blood inside his mouth seems to be a permanent reminder of those awful beatings he suffered at the hands of Susan Grund.

Detective Einhorn once asked Susan if she felt any remorse about the beatings she inflicted on her stepson.

She replied, "Of course I do. . . ." She refused to say anything more about it.

Oklahoma City Assistant D.A. Don Deason, who prosecuted the child battery case back in 1983, says, "Little Tommy's life is ruined. To have killed him might have been more merciful."

In December 1993, further surgery was recommended for Tommy so he could be tube-fed rather than fed orally. He is a curious mixture of adolescence and a child. In many ways, he is much like the toddler he was before those awful beatings battered his brain into submission.

Tommy's grandfather Lester Suenram and his wife visit Tommy every evening at the convalescent home in Bethany. Lester has absolutely no doubts that Susan Grund was probably trying to murder his little grandson for his life insurance when she battered him so brutally.

# Epilogue

**SUSAN GRUND** still is the only one who knows exactly what happened that humid, rainy night in August 1992, and some details could stay locked forever in her memory. Despite intensive psychotherapy in the Indiana State Women's Institution, near Indianapolis, she has never shared with anyone a full account of the death of her husband. She actually insists she is innocent of the charges and is currently writing a book about her life, which she hopes will help her raise additional funds for that appeal against her conviction.

**TANELLE** and **JACOB GRUND** are now living with Jim Grund's sister, Jane and her husband Fred. According to Jane, the children have adjusted remarkably well considering the circumstances, but there is still a long way to go.

**CONNIE** and **JAMES A. GRUND** still live in the same house on Main Street, Peru. Their feelings about Susan have never mellowed, and they visit the grave of their murdered son each and every weekend.

**WIL SIDERS** remains Miami County Prosecutor and still pops into Shanty Malone's bar for a bottle of beer on his way home most evenings.

**ANDY PIERCE** has left his job as a reporter on the *Peru Daily Tribune* to work for a hard-hitting news agency in Chicago.

**GARY NICHOLS** is still a detective for the Peru Police Department and has continued to work on surveillance operations for the FBI and statewide organizations, mainly on drug-related cases.

**BOB BRINSON** continues to investigate homicides countywide for the Indiana State Police, but says he is unlikely, hopefully, ever to find himself at the center of such a controversial case as the Jim Grund murder.

**CHARLIE SCRUGGS** says he is looking forward to retiring from the legal profession and he openly admits that if he could turn the clock back he would have done things a whole lot differently.

**TOM WHITED** has long since abandoned Oklahoma City and all memories of his second wife, Susan. He infrequently sees little Tommy, Jr., and has moved to Texas where he recently qualified as an attorney.

**DARLENE WORDEN** says she will not stop loving her sister Susan despite the murder she committed and the fact that Susan refuses to reply to her letters. But Darlene admits she wishes she had not split the family by informing on her sister to the authorities.

**NELLIE SANDERS** remains convinced that others were involved in the murder of Jimmy Grund besides her daughter. She still lives in the same, rundown house on 3rd Street, Peru; the house that Susan so desperately tried to leave behind forever. . . .

Wensley Clarkson was one of Britain's most sucessful young journalists before leaving London for Los Angeles with his wife and four children in 1991—an experience which inspired his book, *A Year in La La Land*. His other books have included half a dozen best selling true crime books. He has also written biographies of actors Mel Gibson and Tom Cruise. He currently divides his time between homes in London and California. *Deadly Seduction* is his fourteenth book

They'd do anything to win their mother's love.
But would they kill their own sisters?

# *WHATEVER MOTHER SAYS...*

A True Story of a Mother, Madness and Murder

# Wensley Clarkson

Raising her five kids alone in a rundown section of
Sacramento, Theresa Cross Knorr seemed like the ultimate
survivor. But her youngest daughter, 16-year-old Terry, told
police another story. According to Terry, Theresa—no
longer the petite brunette she once was—had turned insanely jealous of her pretty eldest daughters and enlisted the
help of her two teenaged sons in a vicious campaign against
their sisters. Terry's gruesome tale tells how Theresa had
drugged, handcuffed and shot 16-year-old Suesan, allowing
her wounds to fester, until she ordered her sons to burn their
sister alive. Next, according to Terry, her mother savagely
beat 20-year-old Sheila and locked her in a broom closet,
where she would starve to death. Here, in vivid detail, is the
shocking account of Theresa Cross Knorr, a woman who
might just be the mother of all murderesses...

AVAILABLE FROM ST. MARTIN'S PAPERBACKS
WHEREVER BOOKS ARE SOLD

# SLAVE GIRLS

## One of the First Glimpses into the Shocking World of Human Bondage

## WENSLEY CLARKSON

Enter today's sordid world of slaves and masters, where innocent young girls are sold to the rich, and subjected to horrifying degradation. Virtual captives in the mansions of the rich and famous, they risk their lives to tell their stories for the first time.

## A TRUE CRIME CLASSIC

## With 8 pages of revealing photos

**AVAILABLE WHEREVER BOOKS ARE SOLD FROM ST. MARTIN'S PAPERBACKS**

SG 3/01